THE GRANDMOTHER GALAXY

Also by Shirley Ann Ranck

Cakes for the Queen of Heaven (curriculum)
Cakes for the Queen of Heaven (book)

THE GRANDMOTHER GALAXY

A Journey into Feminist Spirituality

by

Shirley Ann Ranck

With a Foreword by Elizabeth Fisher

iUniverse, Inc.
Bloomington

The Grandmother Galaxy
A Journey into Feminist Spirituality

iUniverse books may be ordered through booksellers or by contacting:

iUniverse
1663 Liberty Drive
Bloomington, IN 47403
www.iuniverse.com
1-800-Authors (1-800-288-4677)

ISBN: 978-1-4759-6530-8 (sc)
ISBN: 978-1-4759-6531-5 (ebk)

Library of Congress Control Number: 2012922825

Printed in the United States of America

iUniverse rev. date: 12/10/12

For my children
Scott
James
Christina
Laura

And my grandchildren
Michael
Jacqueline
Camilla
Kevin
Sarah

And my great-grandchildren
Emma
Isabelle
Eric

Contents

Foreword

After reading Shirley Ranck's manuscript, this question occurred to me: *What is the shape of a life?* Shirley retired not too long ago, at the age of eighty, with a deep desire to share her wise woman, or crone, wisdom. *The Grandmother Galaxy* is the outcome. This volume offers us quite a gem—an unusual memoir which provides abundant clues concerning the shape of her life, a gift we should all be thrilled to receive.

Many of us have encountered Shirley through experiencing her course *Cakes for the Queen of Heaven*, her parish ministry or her numerous presentations and workshops. Now she shares autobiographical details about: her time as a child; her parenting of four children, much of the time as a single parent; and her extensive education and multiple careers. Drawing us into memorable moments from her personal life, Shirley also suggests how they relate to her public persona.

Shirley holds three advanced degrees and has had extensive experience in two professional roles: psychologist and minister. During her professional careers, Shirley wrote extensively. We are fortunate that Shirley has included here selections from her previous writings—both academic papers and sermons. She determined they best represent her thinking and feeling about topics that are most important to her.

At times in this book the tone of Shirley's writing shifts as does the nature of her reasoning. This is what I like about *The Grandmother Galaxy*. While the tone and style of her academic writing is markedly different from that of her sermons and reflections, the variety provides a deeper understanding of her multifaceted thinking and philosophy. This mix demonstrates how she chose to participate in life's adventures using varying styles, depending on the circumstances.

Ministry is a unique profession; it is a public life which requires a personal touch. Like artists, ministers in liberal religious traditions often act as catalysts, sharing publically in their sermons a synthesis of their own experiences with what they consider profound from a variety of sources. Through doing so, ministers often change lives. Shirley's sermons do all of this, while positing conclusions that leave room for the listener's interpretation (or, in this case, the reader's) giving them a distinctive conversational quality. The Reverend Doctor Shirley Ranck certainly has changed many lives. *The Grandmother Galaxy* will change many more.

Shirley and I met in the early 1980s before *Cakes for the Queen of Heaven* was published. She had already written the course and collected many images of the female divine. I had just become a Unitarian Universalist myself and was thrilled to find out there was a thriving UU Women and Religion movement; and that Shirley had developed a course to help spread the word about important topics for women. Now this wonderful course has been updated and reissued. Countless *Cakes* groups have taken the course, many continuing as support groups exploring fresh approaches, ritual circles or study groups undertaking other courses.

In the late 1980s Shirley and her work inspired me to take on the writing of *Rise Up & Call Her Name: A Woman-honoring Journey into Global Earth-based Spiritualties*, another UU course which continues to be widely used. The on-going offering of these courses is proof of the importance the Women and Religion movement (W&R) still holds in the UU denomination. Shirley over many years has made significant contributions to this movement. In *The Grandmother Galaxy*, she tells us about her experiences with W&R; she also describes her involvement with both *Cakes* and *Rise Up* over many years of facilitating both courses.

When we met, Shirley was both a psychologist and a minister. She had graduated from Starr King School for the Ministry in the late 1970s, among the first women to attend seminary. Before going to seminary, she had already worked for many years in various settings as a psychologist. At the time we met she was no longer a parish minister, but was deciding whether she wanted to return to ministry or psychology. How she made that decision is one of the revealing stories she shares with us in *The Grandmother Galaxy*.

She did return to ministry, choosing *interim* instead of *called* ministry. In this capacity, over a period of twenty plus years, she served many congregations *in transition* throughout the United States and

Canada. I believe this unique experience gives her sermons a universal quality.

During her master's studies in religious education, Shirley developed an appreciation for Sophia Fahs, an influential Unitarian Universalist religious educator writing in the nineteen thirties and forties. Later she wrote a scholarly paper about Fahs which was published in a prestigious academic journal. Important excerpts from this article are included here: for example, the philosophical underpinnings of a worldview which honors collaboration.

Shirley also carries us into an exploration of post-modern science—which parallels many spiritual and ethical understandings feminist spirituality embraces—making a sometimes difficult topic accessible. Her psychological training and experience also shine through this memoir. Tidbits of insight add counterpoint to humorous stories and delightful pieces of poetry which Shirley has collected in her impressive *medicine bag*.

Because Shirley and I share a deep commitment to women's rights, multicultural experiences, honoring the earth, and women's spiritual contributions, we have kept in touch over the years as she traveled around the continent serving congregations. During these years I have had the benefit of hearing bits and pieces of what is now included here in much fuller detail. The way Shirley artfully exposes the intertwining of the personal and public in her own life provides a model which I believe can aid each of us in seeing the shape of our own lives; and where we might want to go next. *The Grandmother Galaxy* certainly has done that for me.

Treating yourself to Shirley's insights and her wit will make your day both lighter as well as deeper. Getting to know this exceptional woman who has traveled so far, and before many of us had traveled this way, can be just the inspiration you need to *keep on keeping on*.

Elizabeth Fisher
Pacific Grove, California, 2012

Preface

In many places in this country and around the world, ceremonies are being created to celebrate the life passage of women into their years as Crones, as women of wisdom and power. I am a Crone myself and have helped to welcome many women into this important time of their lives. We are the grandmothers, in our work or in our families or both. We are living longer, healthier lives than ever before. We are taking on more and more powerful positions in society, but it is a long and difficult process. We need to be heard, and our society needs to hear us. Our descendants will need to know who we were and what was important to us.

In *Cakes for the Queen of Heaven,* the course and the book, I took on the task of reclaiming women's religious history and its relationship to women's personal lives today. In *The Grandmother Galaxy* I tell more about my personal journey into feminist spirituality and the various issues that emerged as I entered the 21st century. Along with my memories I have included some of my lectures and published articles as well as sermons I delivered over the years. All of these writings give expression to my passions and concerns as a woman, as a psychologist, as a Unitarian Universalist minister. It is one woman's story. It is also my contribution, as a grandmother-Crone, to some of the conversations we must have as we venture into the future.

I wish to express my gratitude to the Unitarian Universalist Women's Federation for honoring me with the Ministry to Women Award and for the feminist theology grant, many years ago, which helped me begin my work on this book. A special thank you as well to Elizabeth Fisher for her editorial expertise, and to all the Women and Religion activists who have helped and encouraged me over the years. Special thanks also to Bob Fisher for helping format the manuscript for publication.

Grateful acknowledgement is made to Rev. David Bumbaugh for permission to quote his article on what Unitarian Universalists believe; to the Unitarian Universalist Association, www.uua.org, for permission to include the Unitarian Universalist Principles and the 1977 Women & Religion Resolution; and to Taylor and Francis (http://www.tandfonline.com) for permission to re-publish "100th Birthday Celebration for Sophia Lyon Fahs" by Shirley Ann Ranck, *Religious Education* Volume 71 issue 6 (November 1976), pp. 603-609. Every effort was made to contact the *International Journal of Women's Studies* for permission to re-publish my article "Points of Theological Convergence Between Feminism and Post-Modern Science," Vol. 2, No. 4, pp. 386-397, July-August, 1979.

Shirley Ann Ranck
Santa Rosa, California 2012

Introduction

I have to cast my lot with those
who age after age, perversely,
with no extraordinary power,
reconstitute the world.

-Adrienne Rich

One summer Sunday a few years ago the church in San Francisco was decorated with brightly colored weavings by a woman artist. They stretched across the wall on either side of the permanent candles lighted up in front, and they flowed down over the ornately carved fronts of the pulpit on one side of the platform and the lectern on the other. In the center, high on a stand in front of the candles stood a shiny brass Goddess from India.

Eight women with fairy dust sparkling in their hair drummed and chanted and danced and spoke their passionate commitment to a spirituality that honors woman, the earth and the contributions of many cultures.

As I sat in the midst of that event I glanced over to the wall on one side of the sanctuary. There carved into the stone were biblical words honoring *the Lord* and *His Kingdom*. And it suddenly struck me that the beautiful Goddess and Her lovely weavings would be moved out after this one service but that *the Lord* would remain there, carved in stone.

When architect Frank Lloyd Wright designed the church in Oak Park, Illinois in 1908, one of his goals was to keep it free of any religious symbols. He almost succeeded. There are no crosses or stars or yin/yang signs. The stained glass uses only motifs from nature. Even the massive pulpit cannot really be called hierarchical in its placement. One third of the people are below the speaker, one third at eye level and one third above. Carved into the stone at the entrance to the building, however, are words about *God* and *man*. In 1908 the great architect was unable to foresee either the humanist or the feminist objections to such words. Nor did he recognize as religious symbols the flowers and plants he used in his stained glass designs.

I begin with these stories of things carved into stone because I think we have many things carved into our institutions and our imaginations. Sometimes it takes a very dramatic event to shock us into changing those carvings. When I was growing up, the phrase "flying to the moon" meant something so impossible that it was ridiculous even to think about it; or it meant a wildly romantic expression of love, as in the old song "Fly Me to the Moon." Only when we actually saw the astronauts walking on the moon, only then did the meaning of the words carved into our imaginations begin to change.

As we continue into this new century, this new millennium, there are at least three areas in which the theological carvings need to be changed. I think of them as imperatives which demand major changes in theology and world view. The first is the feminist imperative which demands that we re-view history and our own thea/ologies so as to begin to include the other half of the story, the female half. The second is the environmental imperative which demands that we pay attention to our sciences and acknowledge our connectedness with other species and all of life so as to bring ourselves into harmony with the life-support systems of this planet. The third is the multi-cultural imperative which demands that we embrace the richness of our racial, ethnic and thea/ological diversity. These imperatives are intertwined in complex ways. Together they demand that we articulate a new world view and a new thea/ology.

Sophia Fahs, Unitarian Universalist religious educator, writing in the nineteen thirties and forties, made important contributions to our awareness on each of these issues. Her work points powerfully toward feminist analyses of personal power and hierarchy, and Gaian concepts of cosmology decades before the women's movement or the environmental movement. Her multi-cultural perspective prepared the way for our Unitarian Universalist acceptance and celebration of diversity.

Becoming aware of the new world view that is emerging will require of us major changes in the assumptions carved into the stone—not only the stone walls of some of our churches but the stone walls of our education and our imaginations. The spiral is one of the great patterns repeated in our universe, our galaxy and our DNA. Growth and creativity do not occur in static repetitive circles as the ancient world believed. Nor do they march forward in a straight line as our 19th century optimists believed. It is necessary to return to the cycles of the past in order to grow. It is also necessary to spiral out beyond these circles into new experiences in order to be truly creative; and the shape of each new event is something more than the sum of all the past events, something truly novel. I would suggest to you that we need to imagine ourselves as The Grandmother Galaxy. That's right! A galaxy full of wise and powerful women!

The image of an old woman is central to each of the three imperatives I have mentioned—a deeply wrinkled, fierce and powerful old woman. I suggest this image to you for the very reason that it is the opposite of what happens in our dominant culture. The experience of most old women is that from about age 40 onward they become more and more invisible, until they are almost completely erased from consciousness. They rarely appear in films or on TV and when they do they are usually portrayed as helpless, ineffective, powerless. Whitney Otto has written a novel, called *Now You See Her*, about this phenomenon of invisibility. In the novel a woman turning forty is aware that people often don't seem to see her. She even begins to experience herself as transparent because as the culture has proceeded to erase her, she has gradually lost touch with her own real self.

Jane Caputi writes, "When I put my ear to the ground, I hear a constant chant: 'The Grandmothers are returning.' . . . We can ignore the behest of the Grandmothers only at extreme peril, for theirs are the Powers not only of the past and the present but also of the future." She suggests that "the truest symbol of the future is the one that our culture most studiously avoids. It is the Crone . . . the most ancient and genuine face of the future. If we are to survive, it is she whom we must most fully honor. It is she whom we must finally and most abundantly become."

We live, we grow and we create a record of our existence as individuals, as a species and as part of the planet. We have as our developmental task the creation of new spirals—new visions, myths and environments for nurturing the life of the human spirit. We can live no longer in the spirals of the recent past, however appealing they seem. And we can deny no longer some distant spirals of the past, however strange they seem. We are destined to create new spirals whether we like it or not, but we can choose what kind of spirals we attempt to create.

The most important thea/ological implication of such a new world-view is that the divine resides not in some supernatural realm but right here in the natural world as the shape of growth and creativity. Life keeps creating new spirals, new events and at each stage, in each event there exists the possibility for novelty.

An individual creates new spirals of understanding on her personal journey. New experiences can cause her to look at the past spirals of her life from a new perspective. In the process a new spiral of understanding may be created. A community creates new spirals of understanding over the course of its history. The spirals of an individual's experience may then interact with those of the community and thus may create new understandings for both the individual and the community. The assumptions of diverse communities may also interact and create new spirals of understanding across old boundaries.

Thea/ologically we face enormous challenges. Can we find symbols in which women and men participate equally? Can we reclaim our ancient matrilineal roots for interaction with our more recent patriarchal past? Can we formulate an ethic in which martyrdom is not admired? Can we imagine myths in which honest human communication is encouraged? Can we discover harmony within us, among us and in relation to the rest of nature? Can we create graceful new symbols and myths in which to carry the complex treasures of our lives?

To begin such a task we need to be aware that we are searching for the universal themes which appear again and again as life unfolds on this planet. Our personal and societal thea/ological spirals are interacting with feminist spirituality; with multi-cultural traditions; and with the implications of the indeterminacies and interdependencies of contemporary science. In the process we may create some truly novel integrations of these many expressions of the human spirit.

As individuals we have felt the impact of decisions, turning points in our lives when we moved into new experiences, gained new insights. Many years ago I was elected vice president of a very large chapter of Parents Without Partners. I arrived at a meeting one night to discover that the president was not there and that I would have to conduct the meeting. As I stood up on the platform and looked out at some 300 people who were eager to get the meeting over with and start dancing, I suddenly realized I had never chaired a meeting, I had never spoken to such a large crowd and I had never used a microphone. It was a moment of frightening new experiences. It was also a moment of growth, as I discovered that I could indeed do all those things.

As members of the human community we can look back over history and see the accumulated culture and accomplishments we inherit, the turning points and events which have shaped our society. As Americans we recognize that our founding fathers granted the vote only to white male property owners. Only with many decades of struggle and a costly Civil War have we grown enough to expand that franchise gradually to non-property owners, African American and Native American men and finally to women. To live means to grow and to change as individuals, as a society, and as a species.

To perceive the divine as growth and creativity immanent in all the world means that the insights of one individual or of one community of faith will not suffice. We can no longer afford to divide the world into armed camps of competing gods and ideologies. We need to look for the common human themes that will enlarge our experience, widen our identities, cause us to grow. In order to discover those universal themes we need to be aware of the unconscious assumptions which are made by all parties or religions, assumptions which few in any of the groups are aware of. Philosopher Alfred North Whitehead put it this way:

"When you are criticizing the philosophy of an epoch, do not chiefly direct your attention to those intellectual positions which its exponents feel it necessary explicitly to defend. There will be some fundamental assumptions which adherents of all the various systems within the epoch unconsciously presuppose. Such assumptions appear so obvious that people do not know what they are assuming because no other way of putting things has ever occurred to them." (in Daly 1973)

Let me cite one glaring example of the way in which our unconscious assumptions prevent us from being truly universal. Until recently we have thought that by giving intellectual acknowledgment to all the major world religions as worthy of respect, by reading occasionally from their scriptures, we were doing all that was needed to express our universal outlook. But because the symbolism of Judaism and Christianity as we have known it is exclusively male and because we assumed that male symbolism was the only kind possible, we failed to understand that the symbols and practices of all of the major world religions as we know them today are patriarchal and tend to denigrate half of the human species.

Let us set all of those traditions aside for a moment and come back to the universal truth that divinity resides in the growth and creativity of all of life, in the growth and creativity of women as well as men. When we look then with new eyes at the major world religions we see clearly that not one of these traditions is adequate for a future in which women participate as full human beings. In the words of 19th century feminist Elizabeth Cady Stanton: "The first step in the elevation of women under all systems of religion is to convince them that the great Spirit of the Universe is in no way responsible for any of these absurdities."(in Daly 1973)

On a personal level then the male view of reality does not foster the spiritual well-being of women. If we are male we may carry with us the idea that our view of reality is the only one possible. If we are female we may carry with us the idea that our view of reality is wrong or unimportant because it conflicts with the prevailing male view. Thus we may perpetuate the assumptions of the past. To tap our divine creativity we need to look at the past with new eyes, with contemporary insights that can help us re-evaluate our experience. It is time we looked at our personal histories from female as well as male perspectives.

As a human community we have also accepted a very biased view of history. For many thousands of years, in historic times as well as in prehistoric times, human beings imagined the divine as female. We have been taught by male historians that the religions of the great goddesses of the ancient world were mere primitive fertility cults. But the archeological evidence of recent years does not support that view. We find instead hymns and liturgies which ascribe to the goddess the power of mighty counselor and the highest demands of love and justice. If we were to open ourselves to female as well as male experience in history we might choose to honor those distant spirals of our human past when the divine was imaged as female. We might then create new stories for a new life.

In seeking a balance between our ties to the past and our openness to the present, we can create something new and beautiful. It is one of the paradoxes of growth that as we take the risk of maintaining creative tensions, we discover new harmonies. In our own psyches, acknowledging our deepest wishes and fears is the first step toward a resolution or constructive use of those forces. In our close relationships a crisis in which resentments are expressed may be the beginning of deeper understandings. In our communities and especially in the world at large we often seem to lack that kind of trust. We pose, we lie, we carry guns, we do everything except meet on a human level and express our common needs for peace, justice, and a sense of meaning and importance. We take mind-boggling risks with our defenses and our lies. Personally we risk our health and destroy our relationships. Politically we indulge in wars. We need to explore new patterns of behavior at all these levels.

In the spirals which follow I will trace some aspects of my own journey into feminist thealogy as the issues of feminism, environmentalism and multi-culturalism touched my life. To express my passions and concerns in these areas I have included some of my lectures, published articles and sermons as well as my personal experiences as a female psychologist and Unitarian Universalist minister. My story unfolds as I describe: my youth and early family life and my marriages and experiences as a single mother; then my interaction with Unitarian Universalism, with post-modern science, with women's religious history, with earth-based traditions and with an increasingly multi-cultural society. My hope is that these spirals may resonate with the thea/ological spirals others have created in their lives. Together perhaps we can create new symbols and stories for feminist thea/ology.

Spiral One—*The Way We Were*, gives some background about my early life, my family and the beginnings of my personal journey into thea/ology.

Spiral Two—*Broken Images and Practical Cats*, explores my excitement in finding not only a new church home but a deepening thea/ological position.

Spiral Three—*Renaissance of Wonder: the Feminist Imperative*, describes my journey into the pre-patriarchal roots of women's religious history and into the wonders of post-modern science—my work at Starr King School for the Ministry and beyond.

Spiral Four—*The Beauty of the Green Earth: the Environmental Imperative*, continues my journey into post-modern science and contains some of my experiences with pagan and earth-based spirituality.

Spiral Five—*A Symbol for Our Times: the Multi-Cultural Imperative*, contains some of my thoughts on the multi-cultural aspects of thea/ology and the symbols needed to express them.

Spiral Six—*Offerings to Hecate*, summarizes some of my thinking and raises some questions for the future.

I have also inserted six short pieces from my newsletter column, Shirley's Cauldron.

The grandmothers are indeed returning and we need the wisdom, the power and the rage of the invisible old women all over the world. We are the future! We are a Megatrend! We are The Grandmother Galaxy.

from SHIRLEY'S CAULDRON

The muse
Ripples the water, opens doors
Lets in sunlight, dazzles and delights.
She frees the poet from all obligations

-May Sarton

It may be that all of us, not just poets, experience the muse occasionally in our busy lives. Some unexpected insight that cannot be reached by the use of our will; a sudden flow of creativity which makes us oblivious to schedules or the need for sleep. There is a kind of freedom that takes over. I used to rush about trying to find time to study or write, saying "I have two hours free on Tuesday so I'll write then." But as May Sarton often points out, the muse cannot be scheduled. Sometimes on that Tuesday I would just sit at one of the big wooden tables in the university library and read poetry or look out the windows at the birds and trees for most of the two hours. And then, out of nowhere, the ideas would come and the writing would begin. Dinner might be late and the baby sitter angry, but I was exhilarated, free "from all obligations." At such times I wondered why I couldn't live more of my life that way—free to feel the presence of the muse and follow her.

Every autumn as the activities of the new church year filled up my calendar, I renewed my promise to myself to allow time and space in order to listen and watch for the presence of the muse. I knew that when I stopped rushing she would release whatever creativity I might possess. May it be so for all of us.

Blessed be!

SPIRAL ONE

The Way We Were

The wonder of being together, so close yet so apart—
Each hidden in our own secret chamber,
Each listening, each trying to speak—
Yet none fully understanding, none fully understood.

-Sophia Lyon Fahs

Chapter 1

My Parents and Me

When I was thirteen I was confirmed in the Episcopal Church in Asbury Park, New Jersey. Impressed with the clarity of the bishop's homily, I made it into this poem which was later printed on the Diocesan calendar.

> "My hands are dedicated to the work of God, the bishop said.
> And as I place them on your head they are not mine but His.
> There are three ways for everyone and this is first.
> He held his hands as if to pray.
> The right hand in the left is next
> For then while at the table of the Lord
> You offer up your self, your soul
> And in return receive His blessing.
> This is given that you may pass it on to all
> By means of hand outstretched in comradeship."

By that time in my young life I had been told many times that prayer was not like asking Santa Claus for gifts (one of my father's pet peeves) but rather about trying to figure out what was right and what was wrong. At "the table" I assumed "the Lord" was Jesus, and I liked the idea that he had touched and blessed his disciples who had then touched others and passed the blessing on through the Apostolic Succession down through the centuries all the way to me. As a very shy girl I felt empowered. I knew I would try to do something good with my life.

Religion was very important to both of my parents. Their views and their personal histories had a great impact on me as an only child. My mother was raised in the Baptist Church in Kewanee, Illinois. As a young adult she rejected organized religion but not the teachings of Jesus. She considered herself a Christian but chose not to join any church. In a way she created her own community. Her personality and her training in journalism made her an excellent listener. She reached out to friends and neighbors in many ways. During the nineteen thirties when a scruffy-looking unemployed man knocked on our door, she would smile and say she had no money but would be glad to fix him a meal.

My father was raised in Jersey City, New Jersey without any church connection, but as a teen went on his own to Old Bergen Dutch Reformed Church. The minister there took an interest in him and encouraged his study of biblical criticism. He also arranged a scholarship for him to attend Hope College in Holland, Michigan and loaned him $100 to get there. At that point in his life my father intended to become a minister.

Independence characterized the early lives of both of my parents. Each was the first in the family to attend high school and later college. My mother was encouraged by her family. My father's family thought he should be working as soon as he finished eighth grade so he completed his secondary education at a night school.

My mother moved to Chicago after high school. She worked as a secretary and attended a city branch of Northwestern University at night to study journalism and drama. After college my father returned to Jersey City. He decided to enter the business world instead of the ministry. A few years later, after the sudden death of his first wife, he was transferred to Chicago where he met and married my mother in 1929. They returned to Jersey City where I was born a year later.

When my father lost his job in the depths of the depression, my mother found an office job. We lived in an apartment in Union City and for awhile a neighbor looked after me and often took me to the park across the street. Ramps to and from the Lincoln Tunnel later replaced the park but not the apartment building. Driving up the ramp from the tunnel some thirty years later I would point to the building and say to my kids, "That's where I lived when I was four." For a few months I lived with various relatives and friends, families in which the men had work and the women were at home. When prohibition was repealed, liquor companies which had been selling alcohol strictly for

4

medicinal purposes were looking to expand. My father landed a job with one and stayed with that company for the rest of his work life.

By the time I was ready for kindergarten my mother was able to quit her job, and we moved to a house in Weehawken. It was there that I made what was perhaps my first conscious independent decision. There were many children on our block and one of my girlfriends had an older sister who was a Rockette. Wow! We had seen the Rockettes dance when we went to the Christmas show at Radio City Music Hall. I begged my parents for dancing lessons and they enrolled me in a tap-dancing class. I practiced hard through an entire school year. In the spring there was a performance by all the dance classes. I danced briefly, a very simple dance with two other girls from my class, and then sat down to watch the rest of the show. Other kids who had started lessons at the same time as I had were featured in elaborate and far more difficult dances. As I watched I realized that even with all my hard work I would never be a really good dancer. So at age seven I said to myself, "I guess I'll do something else." Many years later at a ministers' meeting we played some kind of game where we each wrote down something we thought nobody knew about us. Then we had to guess who wrote them. I wrote that at age seven I had wanted to be a Rockette. While most statements were easily attached to the individuals who wrote them, nobody connected me with wanting to be a Rockette.

Another memory of Weehawken is walking with my mother the two blocks to the boulevard which ran along the edge of the palisades. There we would watch big ships from all over the world come into the New York harbor escorted by the little tug boats. I think I internalized some of my mid-western mother's excitement about this view of a wider world.

As I was growing up I heard from my father the liberal interpretations of scripture that were being suggested by biblical scholars. He was a great admirer of Harry Emerson Fosdick, popular liberal Protestant theologian of the early 20th century. We moved several times as my father climbed the corporate ladder and he would always seek out the most theologically liberal Protestant church in the community. Often it was the Methodist church. He went to church every Sunday and usually taught Sunday school, sometimes adults and sometimes children. My mother was glad to have him take me along so she could enjoy her coffee and the Sunday newspaper.

One of my mother's main objections to organized Christianity was its constant attempts to convert everyone. She seemed to know that other religious traditions might contain just as much truth as Christianity. I never thought to ask her how she knew that. I wonder if perhaps it was her four years of Latin in high school where she read some of the great writers of ancient Rome; or her great love of drama which led her to read some of the ancient Greek dramatists as well as Shakespeare; or perhaps her admiration for the writings of Ralph Waldo Emerson. Whatever path led her to such understanding, I consider it to have been a great theological gift to me as I was growing up in an increasingly multi-cultural world.

Another gift from my mother was a love of poetry. One of my elementary school teachers reinforced that interest by giving her students a large gold star on a chart in our classroom for every poem memorized and recited for the class. I earned a whole long row of stars. Most of the poems are gone from my memory but Wordsworth's *The Daffodils* has stayed with me to this very day. Perhaps it says something about me.

> I wandered lonely as a cloud
> That floats on high o'er vales and hills
> When all at once I saw a crowd
> A host of golden daffodils
> Beside the lake, beneath the trees
> Fluttering and dancing in the breeze.
> Continuous as the stars that shine
> And twinkle on the milky way
> They stretched in never-ending line
> Along the margin of the bay.
> Ten thousand saw I at a glance,
> Tossing their heads in sprightly dance.
> The waves beside them danced
> But they outdid the sparkling waves in glee.
> A poet could not but be gay
> In such a jocund company.

I gazed and gazed but little thought
What wealth to me this show had brought.
For oft when on my couch I lie,
In vacant or in pensive mood,
They flash upon that inward eye
Which is the bliss of solitude.
And then my heart with pleasure fills
And dances with the daffodils.

As an only child moving from place to place every three or four years, friends became very important to me. So did writing letters. In each school I would find a "best friend." When I moved away I would keep in touch by writing letters. Over the years I have lost track of many friends but I am still in contact with some, including Eleanor, my best friend from fifth grade. Now of course we exchange emails, and we are both great-grandmothers.

Methodist churches were usually accepting of my father's rejection of literal belief in the virgin birth or the resurrection of Jesus. My father espoused the position that ancient people ascribed wondrous things to persons they considered especially important, and wrote wonderful stories in which they tried to explain how the world and life came into being. These ascriptions and stories were certainly not to be taken literally by modern people. I remember being surprised as a teen when I encountered people who accepted everything in the Bible as literally true. Learning not to take everything literally was I think an important gift I received from my father. Ironically it was a gift that enabled me eventually to move further and further away from his patriarchal world-view. The old myths might not be literally true for him but they were still empowering to him as a man raised in a patriarchal society. For me the old myths were ultimately not empowering to me as a woman, and could be more easily rejected than stories presented as literal truth.

Eventually Methodist acceptance did not extend to my father's work as an executive for a liquor company. When I was about ten he was superintendent of the Sunday School in the local Methodist Church. A parent complained to the minister, saying that someone who worked for a liquor company should not be superintendent of the

Sunday School. The minister agreed and asked my father to step down. Outraged, my father went to the nearby Episcopal Church and talked with the minister. There both his liberal theology and his employment with a liquor company were happily accepted. He joined the Episcopal Church where he became a Lay Reader and worked with Sunday School and youth groups in that denomination for many years.

I followed my father into the Episcopal Church, often playing hymns on the piano for his Sunday School worship services. It became very much my church. I could listen to the ancient liturgies, easily translating them into modern language and liberal interpretations, thanks to my father's influence. In his later years he drifted away from the Episcopal Church. After I became a Unitarian Universalist minister, he said one time that he thought what he had really always been theologically was a Unitarian Christian.

Music has been a lifelong presence and outlet for me. My father and his brother, Harold, were both accomplished musicians. Harold played the piano and organ. He married into an Irish Catholic family and became the organist at a large Catholic Church in Jersey City. In the days of silent movies he had also played the organ in a movie theater. For someone with no formal education beyond the eighth grade he seemed to have enormous natural talent. He could play any music from classical to popular as well as create sound effects for the movies. He also composed a beautiful waltz for his wife—the Marie Waltz. My father played the violin. He always said he just worked hard at it, that Harold had the natural talent. Watching them and listening to their music over the years I came to doubt that assessment. My father may have had more talent than he thought. As teens the two brothers had earned extra money for the family by playing for parties and dances all around the city. They also had an uncle who was a street musician and spent his days playing his harmonica in Journal Square. When our families got together we spent the entire time making music and singing popular songs. I thought of those gatherings recently when my grown-up grandson invited the family to his apartment where he got us all singing with his karaoke set-up. I learned to play the piano and while I never became as accomplished as my father and his brother, music has always been a source of comfort, an expression of deep emotion, a way of staying in touch with whatever creativity I may possess.

When I was eleven we moved to the shore, to the tiny town of Ocean Grove, one square mile right on the ocean. It was an interesting time to be there, 1941-1945. Ocean Grove is right next to Asbury Park. Whereas Asbury Park had a boardwalk lined with big hotels, shops, rides and amusements of all kinds, Ocean Grove had an unadorned boardwalk with simple benches and lights. Whereas Asbury Park had a big convention hall right on the boardwalk where big bands and pop stars performed, Ocean Grove had a huge auditorium a few blocks inland where famous classical musicians and opera stars came to perform. Ocean Grove was owned at that time by the Methodist Camp Meeting Association. It was supposed to be a place of retreat and relaxation and culture. No liquor was sold and no cars were allowed on the streets on Sundays.

During the war all the big hotels in Asbury Park were taken over by our navy and the British navy. When the big bands played at the convention hall with the windows and doors wide open, there was dancing all along the boardwalk. For girls a few years older than I it was a time and a place for brief sweet-sad war-time romances. Like Humphrey Bogart and Ingrid Bergman in *Casablanca*, or so I imagined. Fifty years later, clips from that movie were still being played in a course I took at the Film Arts Foundation in San Francisco. One night the teacher asked when each of us had first seen *Casablanca*. I said, "When it first came out." There was a shocked silence. I felt very old.

In Ocean Grove during the war, jeeps with anti-aircraft guns patrolled the streets, even on Sundays. The lights along the boardwalk were painted black on the side facing the ocean. But the big wide beaches were still there and my mother and I and my girlfriends spent every day all summer on the beach. We learned to go when the tide was low and coming in. We learned to go out where the waves broke and then ride one in. We got sunburned in June, then turned tan for the rest of the season. The ocean, its sounds and smells, its salty taste became part of me. We stayed in Ocean Grove for four years. I was in high school when we moved inland to Red Bank. We still spent many summer days at the beach or on my cousin's old sailboat on the river.

Sometimes when I look back on a certain period of time in my life, that time seems almost magical. Our three years in Red Bank were like that. My cousin Don had lived with us at times when we were growing up. In 1945 he was just back from serving in the Army Air Corps. He decided to come and live with us again. We all (except my mother of course) joined historic Christ Church in Shrewsbury. There we met Ann, an interesting young woman, a mathematician and ham radio operator who had left college in Minnesota to take a job with the Signal Corps at Fort Monmouth. After church we invited her to come home with us for lunch. When my mother heard that Ann was living in a boarding house, she said, "We have an extra bedroom. Why don't you come and live here?" And she did.

Don and Ann were each as outgoing as I was shy and they made friends wherever they worked or took college classes. Our house was soon filled with veterans and their girlfriends. We met some of them at Christ Church and my father decided to draw all these wonderful young people into a young adult group sponsored by the church. They began to meet regularly, and they persuaded my mother to direct them in producing a play. Other church members got involved in helping with the play. The minister even took a small part in the murder mystery—I think he was murdered in the second act. I was just old enough at 16 to be part of some of these activities. After the meetings and rehearsals of course everyone came back to our house for drinks and snacks and then coffee at midnight. My job was to play popular songs on the piano. My mother also gave me a part in the play. I began to feel quite grown up. I still like to drink coffee at midnight.

Fort Monmouth at that time was taking new recruits into the army and so was full of handsome young eighteen-year-olds—an incredible gift to the local high school girls. One Sunday two young soldiers showed up at our church and were immediately drawn into the gang that met at our house. One of the soldiers, David, seemed delighted to see our baby grand piano. He played beautifully, all kinds of classical music. Ann encouraged me to talk to him. I did and we were soon learning duets on the piano, and more importantly, falling in love. He remained my boyfriend all through high school. I invited him to the proms, and oh my! How my social standing improved when I appeared with a handsome young soldier! We also went out sometimes with Don and Ann and their friends. There was also the big old dilapidated sailboat that Don bought and refurbished so we could all go sailing on the river.

All very romantic. But mostly I think it was all the gatherings at home, the earnest discussions about the future, the romances, the music, the banter that made those years so magical. My sixteenth birthday party was pretty magical too. One of my father's liquor distributors sent us a case of French champagne for the celebration. Another special event was Ann's wedding to one of the handsome vets. They were married at our church, with me as maid of honor, and the reception was at our house. But then Ann was gone, and my own romance ended fairly quickly once we left Red Bank.

In my young mind I think my home had become an extension of my church, or perhaps church was an extension of home. It was all one to me. In later years I sometimes wondered why I couldn't make something like that happen for my children. What I finally realized is that Red Bank was the unexpected coming together of many variables. The war was over and Don, who had always been one of my favorite people came to live with us. The big old house we rented was right in the center of town. Vivacious Ann came into our lives and became my big sister. Fort Monmouth had brought her to our area. And Fort Monmouth was at that time training new eighteen-year-old recruits and so David came into my life. Finally there was an open-hearted church and minister nearby. My parents in different ways both believed that religion was about life and how you lived it. They seized the moment. My father formed a church group where all these young people could not only be together, but also feel that being there together was an important part of their lives. My mother directed a play for them and opened the house to all. Being prepared for company at any time requires not only a lot of work but also some genuine inner motivation. She was a good listener and everyone loved her.

In the decades that followed, whenever any of us happened to meet it was clear that we all remembered the years in Red Bank as a very special time.

As soon as I graduated from high school we moved to Jersey City. My very pragmatic and independence-oriented parents encouraged me to get a job in New York City and to attend the free Jersey City Junior College at night. I found a job at the New York Stock Exchange as a typist and, living at home, I completed my first two years of college at the junior college. My arrangement with my parents was that I would pay for my own meals as we were living in a hotel apartment that had no kitchen. My mother was delighted to be free of the kitchen, although she still made coffee at midnight, in an electric pot. We found several good inexpensive restaurants and only occasionally ate in the hotel dining room. Don met and married a lovely nurse in a lengthy and beautiful Greek Catholic ceremony. At the nearby Episcopal church I met a young veteran and was soon engaged to be married.

Chapter 2

The Problem That Had No Name

In my twenties, married to Phil, a nice young engineer who had a good job, living in a cute little suburban house with an adorable little baby in the nursery, I began to suffer from what Betty Friedan later called "the problem that has no name." I had everything a young woman of that era was supposed to want, even a husband who had encouraged me to finish college at Montclair State Teachers College before we started our family.

In those days it was usual for a husband to support a wife or a family on one full time income, but I had absorbed much of my parents' emphasis on independence. It was important to me that Montclair was inexpensive and I was able to earn enough money for tuition and books by working each summer as a typist. My work at Montclair had included a few months of student teaching, supervised by an English teacher in a Newark high school. One morning I parked my car and went to our classroom where the smiling supervising teacher said to me "I'm changing my mind about you. I just watched you parallel park your car." When I had learned to drive in Jersey City, you had to be able to parallel park really well in order to get your license. The teacher gave me a good high grade on my student teaching, but I wondered if he based it more on my parking skill than my ability as a teacher. Just as I knew at age seven that I would never be a Rockette, I knew at age 22 that teaching high school English and Spanish was probably not the right path for me. I didn't care. I was married and about to start a family. Now that I had graduated and had a baby, why was I restless and mildly unhappy? My neighbors all seemed content with the suburban housewife role, but I was not.

The cute little house was in Madison, New Jersey. One day I put the baby in the car and drove over to Drew University which was right there in town, and asked if they had any graduate programs. They said the only graduate program was the theological school. I went immediately to the theological school office and registered. They put me in the religious education master's degree program. During the next four years I attended part time, had another baby and hired a lovely Mormon woman to baby-sit. My mother took it upon herself to type all my papers even though I was myself a very good typist. I think she enjoyed knowing what I was learning and thinking, but something more happened. We spent more time together and our relationship became more like best friends than mother and daughter.

Mildred Moody Eakin, the only woman on the theological school faculty, was head of the religious education department at Drew and a wonderful mentor during my first year. I remember especially her practicum class. She invited every church in Madison, including the two black churches, to send their nine-year-old children to a several-weeks-long weekday church school. It was held at the seminary in the late afternoon. Experienced teachers were enlisted to do the teaching and we students helped and observed. I don't remember what the content of the lessons was. I know there were songs and stories and activities. The point was to bring children together for some religious education across racial and denominational lines.

After Mildred Eakin retired, Nelle Morton came into the department and became a friend as well as a mentor. It was Nelle who recommended a new book in religious education, *Today's Children, Yesterday's Heritage* by Sophia Lyon Fahs. Fahs influenced my thinking enormously, especially the insights she gained from post-modern sciences. However, I was at that time still fairly comfortable in the Episcopal Church so I never thought to ask what denomination Fahs represented. I assumed I would have to make the same translations and interpretations in any church that I was already making in the Episcopal Church. I learned much later that Fahs always hoped that her curriculum materials would have ecumenical, even inter-faith, appeal.

My work at Drew, and as a part time director of religious education in a local church, gave me an excellent grounding in systematic theology, church history, social ethics, and Bible, including several semesters of New Testament Greek, as well as religious education. I think the only areas I skipped were Hebrew, preaching and missionary work. The Greek classes were memorable. As the only woman in them, I was always called upon to translate St. Paul's most oppressive verses about women.

Another important learning I trace back to those Greek classes concerns distinguished scholars. One of our assignments was to write a paper on all the scholarly ways that one particular Bible verse could be translated and the theological implications depending upon which translation was accepted. I remember sitting at one of the big oak tables in the Drew library as I finished writing the paper. I had studied the way various scholars translated key words and the widely divergent theological implications they suggested. Then I had chosen the scholar whose interpretations I liked best. All these scholars are very distinguished, I thought, but I get to choose the one I like! Somewhat later I learned that the situation was the same in the field of psychology. Many years later in designing the feminist theology curriculum, *Cakes for the Queen of Heaven*, I was careful to choose distinguished scholars to support my views. I knew how top scholars in any field often disagreed with each other, and I knew that I could choose the ones I liked. When the scholarship in the course was challenged by critics, I shrugged. If you want to argue with distinguished mythologist Joseph Campbell or distinguished archeologist Rafael Patai, I said, go right ahead.

Theologically I liked theologian Paul Tillich's use of the terms *ultimate reality* or *ground of being* for the divine. Notice the sense of immanence and the lack of gender. I was fascinated by his attempt to integrate existentialism, psychoanalysis and Christian theology, but his systematic theology did not work for me. He seemed to want the data from these other fields of study to conform to and support an orthodox theology he already had in place. Much later Mary Daly did an eloquent feminist critique of the great theologian and the whole Western religious tradition in her book *Beyond God the Father*. But I was at Drew in the fifties. Along with Sophia Fahs I expected theology to change as new understandings emerged in science or philosophy.

Fahs made her observations and understandings of children central to her theology. If the theology that surrounded her was not healthy for children, she expected theology to change. Turning to contemporary psychology, Fahs emphasized the idea that *how* we gain our beliefs is as profoundly important as the beliefs themselves. There are two main ways of obtaining a set of beliefs or a philosophy of life. One way is to view a philosophy of life as a set of beliefs to be handed down to an individual by some authority. That way one's religion or philosophy of life is a set of affirmations to be learned and accepted as certain truth. The other way is to view a philosophy of life as the product of maturing emotional experiences, meditation and critical thought. Religion then is regarded as the result of your own creative thought and feeling and experience as you respond to life. It was Fahs' conviction that it is healthier to develop a philosophy based upon personal experience. Notice the implication here that the personal experience of women is just as important as that of men. The beliefs of the past and of other people can and should influence that philosophy but not completely determine it.

At Drew I also became aware of the ongoing feud between the older liberal theologians and the newer neo-orthodox theologians. Eventually I knew that for me, whatever the criticisms which could be made about the older liberal stand—mainly that its 19th century optimism was unable to account for the overwhelming evil of the 20th century—I would never be comfortable with the "wholly other" view of the divine, or with old "justification by faith" attitudes which seemed to me to blur the need to work for justice. I saw the neo-orthodox position generally as a step backward.

Two courses at Drew stand out in my memory. One was on theology and the arts. The influence of that course will be evident in some of my writings. The other course was Christianity and depth psychology. In that course I struggled with the concepts of sin and sickness. Do people do evil things because they are by nature bad, or are they just sick? I read the latest writers in psychology and theology and came to the agnostic conclusion that at that point in time we simply did not know. I published my first journal article on this topic. Psychology was the only science ever mentioned in my courses at Drew, except in the book by Fahs. What a paradox! The study of ourselves as human beings kept us trapped in a world-view in which we perceived ourselves as separate individual souls while the post-modern sciences of the material world were discovering the connectedness of everything.

By the time I received my degree in 1958, I knew that I did not want to be a director of religious education. I don't know what I would have thought about being a minister; the idea never occurred to me. I decided to study psychology. Going to graduate school had become my personal solution to "the problem that had no name." I had yet to learn that the personal is political.

Chapter 3

A New Church Home

In the decade that followed I got divorced, remarried, had two more babies, completed a master's degree in clinical psychology at City College in New York City, and a clinical psychology internship at Monmouth Medical Center in Long Branch, New Jersey. At City College I met another young mother who was combining graduate study with giving birth and raising children. We didn't get to know each other well because she lived in the city and I lived in the New Jersey suburbs, but I liked knowing there was another woman on a similar path. Her name was Blu Greenberg and she later became a feminist within Orthodox Judaism. We reconnected briefly many years later when she came to Berkeley, California to give a talk about her feminism. I began then to realize that women, even in the most conservative traditions, were starting to speak up and claim their rightful power.

At City College I also encountered students and professors for whom education was deeply connected to current events in the city and in the world. I used to feel that I couldn't possibly go to a class if I hadn't read at least that day's front page of the New York Times. Professors encouraged lively discussion in class, relating the content of the courses to everything. I remember especially Max Hertzman. As a class ended students would still be engaged in discussion and Professor Hertzman would walk with us to a hamburger place down the street where we continued to talk about the meaning of psychoanalytic concepts. I remember too a class in physiological psychology where I first glimpsed the intricacy of chemical relationships in our bodies, including our brains.

During those years at CCNY I had to make some difficult decisions in my personal life. I had to learn that in some situations no matter what choice you make, someone will be hurt. In the process of getting divorced and remarried I did what I thought was best for my children and for me, but I was estranged from my parents for quite awhile. To them and to many at that time, divorce was something one did only in the most extreme circumstances. They found it very difficult to accept my decisions, or my new husband. My relationship with them was eventually smoothed over but a deep sadness remained and I felt that at some inner level we had lost each other forever. I especially missed the friendship I had with my mother during my twenties. At the time of each of their deaths I remember feeling again that I had already lost them many years before.

My second husband, Jim, introduced me to Zen Buddhism. True Westerners, we did not do Zen meditation or practice any of the Zen disciplines; we read books about Zen, books by Alan Watts and D. T. Suzuki. I did attend a weekend workshop led by Alan Watts and Charlotte Selver. I don't remember any meditation there either, just lectures by Watts and "body work" with Selver. What I took from the experience was the importance of paying attention to my body, to nature, and to the present moment. I was not drawn to meditation, but I was intrigued by the mysterious koans and fascinated by the various disciplines of Zen. Brush painting, or flower arranging or the poetry of haiku. These required lengthy practice until they became a natural part of you. I never tried any of these disciplines. I probably would have said I was too busy. I thought perhaps they would have been something like playing a musical instrument. Something like my experience with the piano. I would practice and practice on a new piece until at last I would say, "Ah, my fingers know it now." At that point I felt free to add feeling or special emphasis to parts of the piece because I no longer had to worry about the notes. And my fingers still know the notes of some classical pieces and some songs. I learned White Christmas when it was new—1942 I think—and now in 2011 my fingers still know the notes even though I haven't seen the music since sometime in the nineteen forties. I don't pretend to understand all that the Zen disciplines do, but some pieces of music certainly became part of me. And I was able then to put something of myself into the music. I wonder if tapping into our own creativity isn't at least a part of what all spiritual disciplines are trying to accomplish.

I remained an Episcopalian for many years, translating the ancient liturgies into modern concepts from psychology or sociology.

I liked Jesus. He was a man of the people. Hung out with publicans and sinners, had compassion for prostitutes, held serious conversations with women. Cared about people. Liked children. Broke the rules if he thought it would benefit someone. I never liked his choosing to be a martyr though. I always thought that maybe someday I would come to understand it but I never did.

I loved Christmas, still do. I can identify with the great event of giving birth, having done it four times myself. It should be celebrated, because as Sophia Fahs says, "Each night a child is born is a holy night."

Easter was no problem for a bright young psychologist. We all experience new life when we struggle through some pain or suffering and rise again.

In short, I had everything neatly psychologized and reinterpreted quite satisfactorily. Except for that martyrdom issue.

All along the way though in my adult life I kept bumping into the facts of my position as a woman. In 1954 I was the only young mother in my neighborhood who was going to graduate school. At the theological school I was the only woman in most of my classes. I thought maybe I was odd.

When I left my second marriage I was on my own for the first time—with four children. I found that life as a single parent was not acceptable or even acknowledged as existing in my church. The women's group met during the day while I was working. At night there was a men's group and a couples club. In the wider community I found that I could not rent an apartment without a male to co-sign the lease. I could not get credit or buy a car. There was no day care for my younger children and reliable baby sitters were expensive if available at all.

I was lucky though. I had stayed in school, first in religious education and then in psychology, so I was able to get a good professional job as a school psychologist. School hours, school vacations, perfect for a single Mom. I was able to get that job because I had insisted upon being an odd ball—a young mother in graduate school.

I began to read the literature of the women's movement and I felt as if a huge burden of odd-ballness was lifted from me. What I had been bumping into was a society not designed to meet my needs as a woman—the problem that had no name. I met other heroic single parent women who were having to start college while working full time as clerks and waitresses and raising the large families so popular in the baby boom years.

I drifted away from the church. I worried that my children were getting a message that religion was not important. Is it important, I wondered? What had kept me in church so long? The ideals of love and justice and a community presumably committed to caring about each other and about the oppressions of this world. I went back to visit the church and for the first time I noticed that little girls were not acolytes, that women were not priests and all the beautiful old liturgies were full of sexist language.

It dawned on me that the authoritarian structures of the hierarchy were rooted not in the teachings of Jesus but in the politics of patriarchy. And just as I was struggling to come to terms with these facts, my church, the Episcopal Church, voted down the ordination of women. They have since reversed that decision. Episcopalians change too. But at the time it was for me the last straw. Reading Mary Daly's *Beyond God the Father,* I saw with increasing horror what most of Western religion had done to women, excluding them from power and at the same time calling them to an ethic of martyrdom. Not because Jesus taught that, but because he did it; and because the churches, composed as they are of human beings, had found it politically expedient to use that ethic to suppress people considered inferior or dangerous throughout history.

I could perhaps have forgiven my church, recognized its human fallibility and worked within it for change. But something had happened inside of me. I realized that my neatly interpreted theology had never really touched the deeper issues of authority, of personal self-worth in the face of overt discrimination, of the psychological unhealthiness of the martyr ethic. I needed to re-think everything. I realized that the personal is indeed political. I began the long process of building a new personal theology.

To express my deepest beliefs and yearnings, a theology would have to value women as well as men. It would have to be democratic in process, and in behavior. It would have to be inclusive in its language and in its attitudes toward all sorts and conditions of people. It would have to be caring in its work. It would have to listen to the sciences and pay attention to what is psychologically healthy. It would have to respect the earth and its creatures and not be about giving *man* dominion over anything.

One night at a Parents Without Partners discussion group we talked about churches and their general lack of acceptance of single parents at that time. Someone mentioned that the Morristown Unitarian Fellowship was fairly open and accepting. I went there the following Sunday with my teen-age son Jim and my two young daughters, Chris and Laura. My oldest, Scott, was already off to college. And so in 1972 I found a new church home.

from SHIRLEY'S CAULDRON

Each night a child is born is a holy night—
A time for singing,
A time for wondering,
A time for worshipping.

-Sophia Lyon Fahs

As Unitarian Universalists we do not celebrate the birth of a divine savior. We rejoice in new life whenever it appears. What then do we celebrate at Christmas? We may wish to honor the birth of Jesus of Nazareth because we respect his teachings. Or we may, with Fahs, proclaim the holiness of every birth. But I wonder if there isn't something more to this special season. In a very real sense, our life on this planet depends upon the light of the sun. The variety of climates in which human beings thrive is made possible by changes in the amount of sunlight that reaches us through the year. This solstice season is about that cycle of light, and the life made possible by the return each year of the sunlight.

We celebrate the longest night of the year, the turning point, the time when reliably every year the days begin to grow longer. Human beings in many cultures have seen this turning point, this return of the light, as a symbol of hope and a promise of new life. In the oldest myths the Sun Child is born, a harbinger of the new life of Spring.

How awesome and how important to remind ourselves of the delicate balance of the earth and sun, which gives us life! May we pause and take note of the light, and may the season bring hope and joy to us all!

Blessed be!

SPIRAL TWO

Broken Images and Practical Cats

In the whole of St. James the smartest of names is
The name of this Brummell of Cats;
And we're all of us proud to be nodded and bowed to
By Bustopher Jones in white spats!

-T. S. Eliot

Chapter 4

Cats!

In spite of my feminism and my thea/ological misgivings, I carry with me a great affection and respect for liberal Christianity as expressed in the Episcopal Church. Maybe because the bishop's homily touched me way back in Asbury Park when I was 13. Maybe because the congregation and the minister were warm and welcoming in Shrewsbury. Looking back, it seems to me however that the church was mainly an expression of my father's patriarchal world. When I entered the big old mansion that housed the Morristown Unitarian Fellowship, perhaps I found more of an expression of my mother's world. She had died of cancer two years earlier. The whole Fellowship mansion smelled of coffee, one of my mother's passions which she passed on to me.

When the service began, someone got up and welcomed everyone, saying that if you were visiting for the first time, please come back a few times because "the same thing never happens twice." That statement was almost literally true. Creative musicians, dancers, poets and artists transformed each Sunday morning into some new and meaningful experience. Paintings, drama, dance. My mother just might have enjoyed it. No hymns, no sermons (even with a full time minister), no prayers, but much that touched and moved people. No theological jargon to translate into modern terms. No candles, no processions. It was a new and exciting experience for me, coming from a liturgical church where you always knew exactly what would happen.

I joined the Sunday Program Committee to learn how these experiences were created. Gradually I began to consider the Unitarian Universalist ministry as a profession I might find more exciting and satisfying than psychology. The course I had taken at Drew on theology and the arts gave me a valuable understanding of the relationship between theology and these various expressions of the human spirit.

My experiences in creative worship at Morristown were important in helping me learn how to communicate that relationship.

When I read that Andrew Lloyd Webber had set T. S. Eliot's practical cat poems to music, I felt vindicated at last. I literally laughed out loud with satisfaction. The best part is that the show became a tremendous hit in London and in New York.

Way back in olden times when I was in college, an English professor suggested to our class that we purchase a collection of T. S. Eliot's work. I bought the book and discovered, among other things, *Old Possum's Book of Practical Cats*. One day I mentioned to the professor how much I liked Eliot's cat poems. The professor stared at me and said, "Of course you know those are not real poetry."

Of course. But as I studied Eliot's serious work and that of other 20th century poets it always seemed important to me that Eliot had also written about Bustopher Jones (above) and the other cats. It seemed exactly right that the practical cats should have emerged a few decades later as a hit musical.

Poets always see their world and their times with a vision that their less observant contemporaries lack. They often see the connections between disparate events, or the overall trends of the culture long before others are aware of them. Or at the very least, poets often gather up the experiences, the fears or the hopes of a generation and give them expression. Eliot, writing in the 1920s and 1930s described the breakdown of all the old securities and beliefs. He saw people struggling to find meaning in a wasteland of broken images. He wrote:

> What are the roots that clutch, what branches grow
> Out of this stony rubbish? Son of man
> You cannot say, or guess, for you know only
> A heap of broken images . . .

Forty years later the theologians caught up with the poet. "God is dead!" they pronounced. God and the entire old order of things has been crumbling ever since. In desperation its leaders, our leaders, cling to their weapons, their outworn ideologies, afraid to let go of the old images, broken though they are, because the new ones are still uncertain and unclear.

Something similar happens very often in our personal lives as well. Take marriages for example. Sometimes we cling to an image of how the relationship should be, pretending to be happy when in reality we are afraid to look at the changes that have occurred.

The playwright Eugene Ionesco takes this pretending to its absurd limits in a scene where a man and woman meet on a train and begin a conversation as strangers. Little by little they establish that they live in the same town, on the same street, in the same apartment building, indeed in the very same apartment. Finally in disbelief they realize that they, two strangers, are husband and wife.

My first marriage was something like that. When I tried to break through the distance that separated us, my husband would become annoyed. One day in a fit of consternation he blurted out, "You are absolutely incapable of getting into any kind of a rut!" I considered that to be a profound compliment.

How does it happen? How do we get so cut off, so distant, so caught up in obligations rather than in the joy of living? I believe there are at least two attitudes or ways of looking at life that contribute to this state of affairs.

The first is living in terms of other people's expectations. I was a good girl. I did well in school, but I never thought to ask what I wanted or needed, only what I was expected by others to do. I buried my needs, and I was angry, but I didn't know why so I tried not to show it. I became distant. I married someone distant. We couldn't afford too much closeness because it might unleash the buried anger and the un-met needs.

The second attitude that contributes to our alienation from each other is living in the future. My in-laws scrimped and saved and denied themselves all their lives so that when they retired they would have the money to fulfill two big dreams—to design and build their own beautiful home and to take a trip to Europe. When they retired they did build a beautiful home in the mountains. They lived in it less than a year when he fell ill and died. The home was too large and expensive for her to maintain so she sold it. And they never did take the trip to Europe. I thought it was the saddest possible way to live and I said, "Not me! I'm going to enjoy life." But not too many years later I heard myself saying to my children, "We'll have more time together after I get my degree. We'll take a vacation when I get a better job, when

I have more money." And there I was living my life in the future too, letting the present slip by unnoticed and unenjoyed. Ric Masten—poet, troubadour and Unitarian Universalist minister—wrote a song about Robert and Nancy that says it well:

> Robert, buried in the Tribune with his coffee, reading all about the day before.
> Nancy, just across the table with her teacup; she studies what the tealeaves hold in store.
> And the now, the moment, slips away; gone with its joy and sorrow.
> He was here yesterday and she is coming tomorrow.

When we live out a stereotype, meeting other people's expectations, we shrink ourselves and ignore our own human needs. We cannot be open to the present lest our needs and our anger show. We feel distant, trapped, and life passes us by. When we live in the future instead of the present we lose contact not only with other people but with nature as well. We have no time for flowers or sunsets in our drive toward the future. We can also ignore pollution. We wind up with neither people nor nature to sustain us.

Why does it happen? What are we afraid of in the present and in ourselves? One time in Morristown the minister of the Fellowship called me early Friday morning before I left for work. "Shirley," he asked, "Can you speak Sunday morning for one minute on psychological truth?" "Psychological truth in one minute?" I said, "Sure!" He invited a poet, a scientist, a painter, a musician and me, a psychologist, to speak on our particular brands of truth. When we got together on Saturday to share what we planned to say we were struck by the fact that we all mentioned a moment of terror, of profound anxiety. The artist facing a blank canvas, the individual in therapy having to let go of an old self in order to face who she might become, the scientist proposing a new hypothesis—all face that moment of terror.

I believe there are moments in all of our lives when we must break with the shattered images and worn out ethics of the past and put forth our own perceptions of the world, our own true thoughts and feelings and actions. Moments when we risk the anger of our families or the strictures of our society in order to be our authentic, healthy selves. At such moments we may feel we are on a cold journey in the dark, all alone. It is no wonder we often squelch our real selves rather than risk loss of relationship, social ostracism or in some cases even violence.

For most people today God is dead, heaven is an illusion and hell is here and now. T. S. Eliot labeled the situation well when he called it The Wasteland. It is indeed terrifying to live in a wasteland, where all the old securities have become a heap of broken images.

In Eliot's time and for many years thereafter it was fashionable to assume that we were helpless victims of forces beyond our control. Individually we were envisioned as driven by unconscious impulses, and socially we felt at the mercy of political and economic powers. There appeared to be nothing we could do to extricate ourselves from the wasteland of modern life.

Poets and artists have long been pointing the way toward a new image for humanity. Eliot understood that whatever that new world-view might be, it would at least in part be a reclaiming of our origins, our sources, our beginnings. He writes in Little Gidding:

> We shall not cease from exploration
> And the end of all our exploring
> Will be to arrive where we started
> And know the place for the first time.

Today we have it spelled out for us by psychologists who implore us to elevate trust, nurturance and relationship to a place of greater importance than distrust, conquest and alienation; and by ecologists who beg us to halt our exploitation of the earth, to return to an understanding of nature as sacred. Return, they say, to those human qualities we have neglected and to that connectedness with nature that we have all but lost.

The practical cats always knew who they were, what they wanted and what was important. Part of their appeal lies in the very fact that we know cats refuse our anthropomorphic projections. They simply go about the serious and hilarious business of being cats. For a long time now we humans have not known who we are. A popular song a few years ago put it succinctly: We didn't know who we were; we were just on the road. Even earlier the Beatles sang about the nowhere man who doesn't have a point of view, and knows not where he's going to.

Wallace Stevens in his poem *Sunday Morning* describes a woman enjoying a Sunday morning breakfast on her porch with the smell of coffee and oranges and the colors of a cockatoo in the sunshine. But then the shadow of past religious teachings crosses her mind and the poet, affirming her need to move beyond those teachings, writes:

> Divinity must live within herself . . .
> All pleasures and all pains, remembering
> The bough of summer and the winter branch.
> These are the measures destined for her soul.

Psychological Truth In One Minute

Psychological truth often appears to be illogical and irrational. I may feel miserably unhappy; you may look at my life situation and say that objectively, rationally, I have good friends, a pleasant family, money, everything that should make one happy. But my psychological truth is that I am miserable. It doesn't help much that you say I'm irrational. Why is there such a gap between your objective observations and my feelings? Because psychological truth is made up of many unseen variables. Besides a person's present life situation and its complexities, there may be physiological difficulties, or there may have been past experiences which are still affecting present behavior and attitudes. What makes my behavior and attitudes seem irrational is that you and I both may be completely unaware of these unseen variables. Yet they are very real and constitute my psychological truth.

Coping with such unseen and unfelt variables involves becoming aware of them. The paradox or the religious aspect of psychological truth is that in order to understand another person's seemingly irrational behavior, you must first become aware of your own history and your own body. It can be scary to find out that you don't like the person you have become because that's you, the only self you know. If you give up that self maybe you won't have any self at all. But right at this terrifying point there is the realization that it may be possible to become a new and different self. So you begin to do battle with your personal demons—in my case clumsiness, shyness, and an overwhelming sense of inadequacy. Understanding how we got to be who we are is the first step, looking back into our personal histories.

But giving up that old self is the hardest part. Most of us have to struggle a long time. We cling to the old feelings and the old ways of behaving. I believe that we find the courage to try new ways when there is an enabling relationship with another person. Within the context of such a relationship we can face and understand and forgive our own irrationalities, and we can risk losing that old self in order to find a new identity. Then when we look around at the behavior of others the words of the popular religious song become very true: "Take a look at yourself and you can look at others differently." Differently meaning with more compassion and understanding of the many unseen variables that make up psychological truth.

Chapter 5

Candlesticks, Beer Cans and Fortune Cookies

As a very shy person, one of my big concerns was always communication. In the aftermath of two divorces and in considering an adventure into a new profession, I felt a need to do some serious psychological soul-searching. I began by pondering these words by e e cummings:

> be of love (a little)
> more careful
> than of everything

My second husband, Jim, had been married and divorced twice before he married me. He was also raised in China and loved Chinese food, so over the years we went to many Chinese restaurants and opened a lot of fortune cookies. One night he broke open the cookie, and read "You are doomed to be happy in marriage." He kept that little scrap of paper taped to his desk for years. We were later divorced, and he married a fourth time.

In his work as a clinical psychologist, Jim did a lot of marriage counseling and he always made it clear to a couple that his commitment was to the growth and fulfillment of the individuals rather than to the saving of the marriage. If the marriage contributed to their individual well-being, he was all for saving it but if it did not, he felt that separation might be the healthier path. In his own life, committed as he was to personal growth, he was doomed on the one hand to a lack of permanence in marriage, but on the other hand he enjoyed a great zest and enthusiasm for each new relationship.

The tragedy for many couples in the past was that they went on maintaining the appearance of a marriage even though the relationship had long been lost. The tragedy for Jim and for many of us today is that our healthy refusal to maintain phony appearances finds little support in our ceremonies and rituals and customs which still tend to celebrate permanence at the expense of individual growth.

For several years I was part of an ongoing discussion group within the organization Parents Without Partners. Over and over, divorced people, after they had drained off their anger and resentment, would get around to saying: I guess I still care about my ex-husband or ex-wife, but we never expected each other to change. There was nothing in the wedding ceremony about that. We expected to stay the same. There usually followed a realization that although the marriage could no longer work, it had not necessarily been a failure if it had contributed to their personal growth.

I feel that way about both of my marriages. Both were relationships that enriched my life and contributed to my growth as a person each for a decade or more. I don't think we failed. I think we just grew and changed in ways that made our particular relationship unworkable. In the discussion group, however, there were many evenings when we ended with the question: What if our expectations had been different?

It seems to me that the underlying issue here is whether personal growth and fulfillment must necessarily be opposed to permanence. Divorced people like me tend to make a virtue of growth and to minimize the importance of permanence. People who have stayed married for many years tend to make a virtue of permanence and to minimize the importance of growth. I believe this is a false dichotomy. Many couples have only the appearance of permanence; the relationship is lost. And many of us who decide to end a relationship fail to learn or grow from the experience and may repeat the same self-defeating patterns in a new relationship.

When a relationship is alive and contributing to the well-being of both persons, there is communication. Unfortunately men and women in this society still exist in a relationship structured in ways that often interfere with authentic communication. Men have been taught to feel it is a sign of weakness to have to express their needs; they often expect women to know and meet their needs automatically. Women for our part are not encouraged to take our own needs seriously, much less express them. We are taught instead to focus on the needs of others. So we may have two people, each expecting the other to know what they need without ever having to state their needs in any straightforward way.

The problem is that in order for me to tell you what I need, I have to know myself pretty well first. But the way that we are raised as males and females does not really foster that kind of self-knowledge. As Jean Baker Miller points out, women are encouraged to believe that if they do go through the struggle of self-knowledge and self-development, the result will be disastrous—they will forfeit the possibility of close relationships with men. To avoid this, women are diverted from exploring or expressing their needs. They are encouraged instead to see their needs as if they were identical to those of others, either men or children. Women may at first feel selfish and guilty when asking for what they need. Men often become confused and angry when their needs are no longer automatically taken care of, and they may at first feel humiliated by having to ask for what they need.

But when we are able to set these stereotypes aside, when there is a real sharing of deepest feelings, longings, hurts and joys, there is excitement and learning and growth. It is not enough to care deeply; love requires authentic expression. And it is in the communication, in the sharing that we discover ourselves and each other. e e cummings says it this way:

> we are so both and oneful
> night cannot be so sky
> sky cannot be so sunful
> i am through you so i

This experience of heightened self-awareness has been for me a characteristic of close friendships perhaps even more than of marriage. I have two or three friends with whom there is a trust and an understanding that transcends all differences of attitude, opinion and lifestyle. These friendships have been far more permanent than my marriages. Of course, my friends don't have to live with me. We get together when we are motivated to do so, sometimes infrequently. I have always thought that Gibran had the right idea when he said "Let there be spaces in your togetherness." What makes for quality in a relationship is the authenticity of our communication.

There is a sad old song which says "You don't bring me flowers anymore." It isn't just a matter of remembering the other person's needs. We have to have the courage to state our own needs and the wisdom to know when to stand firm in getting those needs met and when to set our own needs aside temporarily in order to give the other person room to grow.

This wisdom is especially important in our relationships with children. Good parenting of very young children requires that we put their needs ahead of our own much of the time. But if children are to grow and to relate to others successfully, we must somehow teach them that those others have needs and feelings that must be considered. And of course if we parents are to survive as persons in relation to our children, we have to communicate our needs and feelings to them more and more as they grow up.

In marriage, in friendship and in our relationships with children, it is communication that determines both the growth and the permanence that will be found in a relationship.

We come now to the candlesticks and beer cans. Many years ago when my first husband and I moved to a little house in the suburbs, we started attending a local church. One evening a woman came to see me about joining the women's group at the church. Now I was a very serious and shy young woman. I felt that people should spend their free time doing important things for society. The lady who came to see me told me what a wonderful time the women had in her group. The last time we got together, she said, we made candlesticks out of old beer cans! The incident became for me a symbol of the kind of meaningless life I wanted to avoid. Just as the relationship between two people can be lost in the absence of authentic communication, so too can the real depth of community be lost in a group when there is no real sharing of ultimate values. The symptom in groups is often a flight into meaningless activity.

I began to notice years ago that there were some social situations in which I could hardly function at all. I just could not seem to learn to make conversation. In other situations, I felt somehow more at ease and I would find myself talking freely in heated discussions. For a long time I was puzzled. I could not seem to pin down just what it was in some situations that made me uncomfortable. What I finally realized was that it was a matter of the kind of communication that took place.

When people hid behind a mask of niceness, I would retreat into my own shell and wonder why there was nothing to talk about. When people were open and shared their real thoughts and feelings, I would do the same and our conversation came to life.

The single parent discussion group I mentioned earlier was like that. We had a real depth of community. There was one member of the group I always thought of as Eeyore in *Winnie the Pooh*. The gloomy depressive donkey who can see only the negatives in any situation and is always pessimistic. That's how our group member was so I'll call him Eeyore.

Our group met every Tuesday night and Eeyore was always there. He not only came every time but he was always the very first person to arrive. He would sit down in a big comfortable chair and slouch down as low as possible. He kept his balding head down through the entire discussion, glancing up perhaps once or twice during the evening to make some gloomy comment. The group accepted him in all his misery. And gradually we learned that he was a deeply grieving widower with a little girl to raise. As the weeks and the months went by, his head came up a little more often and he didn't slouch down quite so low in the chair.

Then one night I saw him at the big general meeting of the chapter. Now one of the problems for people when they joined our large chapter of Parents Without Partners was coming to the general meeting for the first time. You walked into a huge hall filled with 300 to 400 people. You didn't know anyone. And many people turned around and went home the first time they tried it. Those of us who were leaders in the chapter tried to find ways to welcome people and help them get acquainted. We had orientation tables set up near the entrance and members there to greet new people and answer their questions. It was a job I would never have expected Eeyore to take on. But there he was, behind one of the orientation tables, and he was smiling! And talking to a newcomer. As I walked past the table, I overheard him saying "You might try one of the discussion groups. It really helps."

Authentic communication is at the very heart of love. It is crucial not only in our close personal relationships, but also in our community. It was this community aspect of communication which ultimately pushed me toward ministry and away from one-on-one psychology. Raymond Baughan has written:

> Here in the space between us and each other
> lies all the future
> of the fragment of the universe
> which is our own.

Chapter 6

Tigers!

In those busy days in the middle of my life I sometimes felt trapped among the "tigers" in my life—my children, my work, my home, our pets, the long slow one-course-at-a-time path toward a doctorate—like the man in this Zen koan: A man traveling across a field encountered a tiger. He fled, the tiger after him. Coming to a precipice, he caught hold of the root of a wild vine and swung himself down over the edge. The tiger sniffed at him from above. Trembling, the man looked down to where, far below, another tiger was waiting to eat him. Only the vine sustained him. Two mice, one white and one black, little by little started to gnaw away the vine. The man saw a luscious strawberry near him. Grasping the vine with one hand, he plucked the strawberry with the other. How sweet it tasted!

Looking back on that time I would say that the berry did indeed taste sweet. I was in the midst of another somewhat magical time in my life. I had a good interesting job. I was able to buy a small house in Florham Park. My children were all doing well in school and we enjoyed some good family times. There were also interesting new people in my life—colleagues from work, members of the Morristown UU Fellowship, and members of Parents Without Partners. One of the PWP discussion groups met at our house and I began to have occasional parties when friends from all these places met each other. Once again the coming together of diverse variables made for a feeling that life was good no matter how busy.

I also saw some connections between Zen and Unitarian Universalism.

Unitarian Universalists used to have a koan we presented to the world and to ourselves in the form of a bumper sticker. It said, "To question is the answer." That statement is as baffling to most people as the Zen koans are to us. And if we were each to write down our own interpretations of it, we would surely have a great variety of meanings. And yet when we saw it on a bumper sticker we would smile a smile of recognition. We knew. What did we know?

I believe we knew that at some point we, and that person in the car with the bumper sticker, at some point we felt everything we knew or thought we knew was torn down and called into question. At that point we discovered ourselves. We started on the long journey toward our own natures, looking within instead of outside ourselves for the resolution to life's ultimate questions. We found an exhilarating new freedom in our questioning and in our sense of selfhood.

I would suggest to you that this questioning we do and our elusive responses to the questions of newcomers, that all of this is a point of contact with the way of Zen. When someone asks you "Now just what do Unitarian Universalists believe?" Or "What must I believe to join your church?" you may feel a fair amount of empathy for the Zen masters who sometimes hit their students over the head with a stick or knocked them to the ground. At the very least you may feel like shouting "Who are *you*?" "What do *you* believe?" Because you know that just as important as the beliefs themselves is the discovery that *you* must find your own. That's what we know and that's what we know about the person in the car with the bumper sticker that says "To question is the answer."

It is important to understand that we are not talking only of psychology, of healthy rational consciousness which challenges authority and demands empirical evidence. What is involved is an awareness of the human situation, an ultimate question about the source of meaning in our lives. It is our very human consciousness which causes us to wonder, to question. But it is that very same consciousness and rationality that can keep us from being ourselves. In Western culture we tend to look at everything as objects. We even want to examine our selves as objects and in doing so we can cut ourselves off from the very real subjective experience of selfhood, of awareness of our own depths, of trusting our own subjective experience as valid, as the source of meaning.

D. T. Suzuki suggests that even our Western poets are often objective and analytical. To illustrate he compares a Japanese poet with Tennyson. He writes: "Basho, a great Japanese poet of the seventeenth century, once composed a seventeen-syllable poem known as Haiku. It runs, when translated into English, something like this:

> When I look carefully
> I see the nazuna blooming
> By the hedge!

"It is likely that Basho was walking along a country road when he noticed something rather neglected by the hedge. He then approached closer, took a good look at it, and found it was no less than a wild plant . . . The poet can read in every petal the deepest mystery of life or being.

"Let me see now what the West has to offer in a similar situation. I select Tennyson. His short poem here quoted has something very closely related to Basho's.

> Flower in the crannied wall,
> I pluck you out of the crannies;
> Hold you here, root and all, in my hand.
> Little flower—but if I could understand
> What you are, root and all, and all in all,
> I should know what God and man is."

Suzuki goes on to say: "There are two points I like to notice in these lines: First, Tennyson's plucking the flower and holding it in his hand, root and all, and looking at it, perhaps intently . . . the difference between the two poets is: Basho does not pluck the flower. He just looks at it . . . As to Tennyson, he is active and analytical. He first plucks the flower from the place where it grows . . . which means that the plant must die. Second, Tennyson . . . proposes the question 'Do I understand you?' Basho is not inquisitive at all. He feels all the mystery as revealed in his humble flower . . . Tennyson's individuality stands away from the flower . . . His understanding tries to be objective. Basho is subjective. Basho and Tennyson are indicative of two basic characteristic approaches to reality."

Even our Western sciences now have come to acknowledge the role of the experimenter as an interacting part of the total environment being studied, so one can never be entirely objective. Both Zen and

Unitarian Universalism would have us find life's meaning in asking the ultimate questions for ourselves and in so doing discover our true selves, our subjective as well as our objective selves, our Buddha natures, our divinity.

As Unitarian Universalists we often bewail the fact that although we can articulate all kinds of religious attitudes and beliefs that we reject, we have some difficulty saying just what we affirm. It is interesting that Alan Watts begins one of his books on Zen by saying that Zen is a way of liberation which can have no positive definition. Instead it has to be suggested by saying what it is not, somewhat as a sculptor reveals an image by the act of removing pieces of stone from a block. It is very important to do the work of stripping away all the layers of authority and dogma, of inherited structures and beliefs, to get down to the basic religious questions we all experience: Who am I? And what is the real meaning of my life?

Our difficulty is in describing just what it is that happens when we begin to ask those existential questions. We experience something which is perhaps similar to what in Zen is called enlightenment. Something happens in a moment which illuminates all our questions in a way that just thinking couldn't achieve. It seems that as we attend to who we are, we open ourselves to the nature of others, both human and non-human. We see ourselves in them and we see them in ourselves. We discover that we are connected, that we are all of one nature. We discover that enlightenment, the divine, is nowhere if not within us and within the world of our everyday lives.

We diverge most from Zen perhaps at the point of discipline. We question, we turn inward, we experience some genuine insights. But our process is sporadic and we escape into intellectual evasions more often than we should. We have not developed art forms or ceremonies which would allow us to express our insights and open the way for further learning.

According to D. T. Suzuki, Zen has to do with becoming the artists of our own lives, with behaving truly to oneself. The Zen of Unitarian Universalism is our continuing discovery of our true natures.

from *SHIRLEY'S CAULDRON*

Years ago a cartoon made the rounds among psychologists. Two rats are in a Skinner box and a human researcher is approaching. One rat says to the other, "Boy have I got him well trained! Every time I hit that lever he puts food in my dish." Then there was the cartoon character Yogi Bear who knew exactly where to find the picnic baskets of hapless campers. We used to think such animal cleverness only happened in cartoons. We thought they were funny.

One summer, high in the mountains near Dillon, Colorado my friends and I drove to a scenic spot where many people come to feed the squirrels. We took along a bag of pistachio nuts—only the ones we couldn't pry open with our fingernails. We planned to let the squirrels have them. As we stood at the scenic spot and started to put the nuts down for the squirrels, a little girl beside us said, "Oh they won't eat those; they only take the ones that are easy to open." She was right. The fat little squirrels turned up their noses at our tightly closed pistachios and scampered away to find better offers. These real squirrels had these humans well-trained indeed!

On the beach at Pt. Reyes National Seashore my family and I stood in the fog at the edge of the ocean, bundled in sweatshirts, but numbing our toes in the cold water. Suddenly my daughter, Chris, screamed and went running up the wide beach toward our blanket and possessions. We turned to see a huge seagull systematically pulling plastic bags of cookies and crackers out of our beach bag. By the time Chris reached the blanket the gull had pecked enough holes in a bag of Oreos to make off with one cookie and dump the rest into the sand—for future snacking no doubt.

So who's training whom? I have long been proud of our UU seventh principle affirming "the interdependent web of all existence of which we are a part." But I didn't realize that seagulls have now acquired a taste for Oreos.

Blessed be!

SPIRAL THREE

A Renaissance of Wonder: the Feminist Imperative

We do not want a piece of the pie.
It is still a patriarchal pie.
We want to change the recipe.

-Rosemary Matson

I am awaiting
perpetually and forever
a renaissance of wonder.

-Lawrence Ferlinghetti

The feminist imperative is the one that says that women and men are created equal in value. If wise old women were visible and powerful, perhaps we would all be well-educated about the female half of our religious history. Whatever attitude or belief you may hold about God or the divine, it is a symbol that is a powerful part of our human heritage. In our dominant culture we grow up hearing this symbol spoken of only in masculine terms such as *Lord* and *King* and always referred to with masculine pronouns. In the last thirty years a growing number of women and men have been trying to change that by using inclusive language. But just a few years ago, at a colloquium at Starr King School I had to speak up and object to the use of exclusively male language for the divine in the worship services. And just last year at a conference of Unitarian Universalist ministers, it happened again! Three readings in one service referred to God in exclusively male language. I left the room.

Apparently most of us still don't know that for many thousands of years human beings, men as well as women, imagined the divine as female. In later times human beings imagined great pantheons of gods and goddesses. Eventually as we know from recorded history the male gods grew more and more powerful and became the chief deities in the pantheons. In our Western tradition, however, the Great Father replaced the Great Mother. Even if we are humanists we need to understand what that has done to our thinking, our language, our institutions, all of which reflect this assumption that the male is God. The mythology of a culture reflects its social arrangements. When you have a myth of God the Father and God the Son with barely a mention of any female, even the humanists in that society will carry an assumption of male supremacy. We need to keep examining our behavior and the assumptions which are still carved into our imaginations. Unexamined assumptions can affect our behavior even when our conscious intentions are good.

Who are the old women in your life? How well do you know them? Are they powerful?

Chapter 7

A Birthday Celebration

In 1976 Sophia Fahs celebrated her 100th birthday. My old friend and mentor, Nelle Morton, called and asked if I would like to write an article about Fahs for the journal *Religious Education*. To write such an article was an exciting opportunity for me to spell out and celebrate the theological views Fahs had presented, views that were central to my own theological journey. Fahs was a woman who, I believe, pointed the way to the future for feminist thealogy and for Unitarian Universalist thea/ology. A woman who stood on the threshold between the old world-view of patriarchy and violence and an emerging scientific world-view of cooperation and peace. Well-known as a leading Unitarian religious educator, she created a renaissance of wonder for many hundreds of children and teachers of religion. I would suggest to you that she was also a major thea/ologian, perhaps not recognized as such because she was a woman. In June of 1976 I attended the General Assembly of the Unitarian Universalist Association in Claremont, California and participated in the Fahs birthday celebration.

Hundreds of white balloons floated in the warm California night, candles flickered, and champagne corks popped all around as the Liberal Religious Education Directors Association gathered for the party. There was a huge birthday cake and the party goers sang and danced well into the night. Some even danced barefoot in the shallow pool in the center of the courtyard where the party was held.

To open the party, members of LREDA with the Reverend Alan Egly of the Community Church in New York City as Master of Ceremonies celebrated some of Sophia Fahs' accomplishments. Fahs was toasted with champagne three times during the program, first for her great trust in and commitment to children and their need to grow freely, second for her many curriculum materials, and third for her use of many forms of creative expression in celebrating life's special moments. Words, music and movement were used to express some of the content of Fahs' work. Perhaps the most delightful presentation was that of Barbara and Hugo Holleroth who greeted each other with "Martin!" "Judy!" and proceeded to take the roles of Fahs' well known curriculum children as if now grown up and looking back on their days as playmates.

At the end of the program several people told personal anecdotes about their contact with Sophia Fahs and as the candles were lighted on the cake, a letter from her was read expressing her appreciation for the party and her wish that she could be present.

It was a good party and the program gave genuine recognition to Fahs for her many curriculum materials, for her tremendous insight into the religious needs of children and for her creative innovations in worship for children. Her prophetic theology, however, was scarcely mentioned. Perhaps a party was not the appropriate place for a serious theological discussion. Another way to celebrate her birthday might be to re-examine the writings of Fahs today as a source for a new world-view, and for new myths which may be able to heal the schizoid quality of our culture.

Fahs seems always to have applied a pragmatic test to inherited religion. Having the courage to trust her own experience, she seems to have decided that if the religion she received did not fit in with her own experience it was the religion that had to change. As a young woman this principle enabled her to see that writing to her fiancé on the Sabbath was a true rest for her despite her mother's disapproval of Sabbath letter writing. Later as a religious educator the same principle allowed her to view the Bible as the record of one ancient people among many and to deprive that tradition of its superior status. Fahs turned to the findings of the 20th century physical and behavioral sciences to find myths and symbols relevant to her life.

Emerson commented in 1879 that "the venerable and beautiful traditions to which we were educated are losing their hold on human belief, day by day . . . The old forms rattle and the new delay to appear . . . The mind, haughty with its sciences, disdains the religious forms as childish. In consequence of this it appears as the misfortune of this period that the cultivated mind has not the happiness and dignity of the religious sentiment . . . We are born too late for the old, and too early for the new faith." (in Fahs 1965) It has been Fahs' conviction that it is no longer "too early for the new faith."

The fragmented, alienated quality of the modern human predicament has been repeatedly described by social critics and by artists. Rollo May went so far as to suggest that the most widespread personality pattern in our culture is the schizoid one, the divided one in which thinking and feeling have become separated. Picasso's painting, Guernica, is perhaps the classic example of the artistic representation of the fragmented, alienated, warring nature of life in the 20th century. Male theologians have not seen the biblical tradition as undergirding or contributing to this condition. They have instead held fast to that tradition as a means of overcoming the alienation. Early 20th century theologians wanted to know the historical Jesus and apply his ethic. Neo-orthodox theologians interpreted our alienated predicament in terms of the biblical fall, offering a leap of faith in a "wholly other" God or Ultimate Reality as the healing answer. Even the death of God theologians remained within the biblical realm; why else would it be necessary to pronounce the biblical God dead?

Fahs suggests that the divisive authoritarian structures that pervade our society and dominate our thinking are rooted in the biblical cosmology and morality. Our theological options have been a neo-orthodoxy which reaffirms the biblical tradition, or an ineffective humanism in which God is dead but people, lacking a sense of wonder, are still unconsciously caught in his divisive dualistic world-view. Fahs observed children and found that they were curious about life and that the questions they raised were similar to those raised by people of all cultures, the same questions which gave rise to the great religious writings of the past. She suggests that it is this same wondering about life that in our time motivates the scientist. She turns to science for indications of a new cosmology and a new morality. She was aware that religious liberals feel that they have rejected the ancient pre-scientific view of the universe even if they remain committed to certain truths in the Bible. Fahs points out that we have not been aware of all the aspects of such a cosmology, and that when it is truly rejected, certain so-called truths are also called into question.

The particular relevance of Fahs today lies in the concern expressed by scientists themselves about the uses made of their findings. Bevan deplores the lack of public understanding of science and suggests that we need to evolve a world-view that integrates our fragmented and many-faceted experience. He goes on to insist that it cannot be a philosophy of unlimited physical and psychological exploitation. His reason is that we have explored the ends of this earth and the very science and technology that many now condemn have made it clear that there are limits and how close we are to reaching them. He points out that the richer, fuller, more meaningful life that the vast majority of us seeks requires that we have a more coherent view of the world. This understanding must include an understanding of ourselves and of our place in nature. He suggests that a broad understanding of science is the only means to this end. The task he sets before us is a theological one, understanding ourselves and our place in nature, developing a coherent world-view. Fahs is a theologian who agrees that a broad understanding of science is the means to that end.

Fahs (1952) took on a double task, first pointing out the ways in which the biblical cosmology still pervades our thinking and our social structures, and second gleaning insights from science upon which to base new thinking and new social structures.

One aspect of the biblical cosmology which still affects us is the idea that creation was totally completed at some point in the past and remains fixed and unchanging. We are taught the biblical story and we grow up expecting our world to be changeless. But we do not experience life as fixed and unchanging. Consequently we are in a constant state of future shock. Fahs suggests that if we look to our own modern science we will find evidence for a cosmology that is much more in tune with our experience. There is evidence for example that the universe is continually growing and expanding, that new matter is coming into being and that new species of animals continue to appear. Evolution is no longer seen as the result of chance mutations. There is instead a recognition of a creative process within organisms themselves.

The biblical cosmology also projects a clear-cut distinction between the natural world and the spiritual world, with the natural world seen as degraded and inferior. People are seen as living in two distinct places, the temporal material world and the eternal spiritual or supernatural world. These two worlds are seen as enemies. The world and the flesh are evil and in the story of the fall there is a curse upon nature. Human beings are condemned to struggle against the natural world and to conquer it. If we face squarely what is happening to our natural environment today, it is all too clear that we are still operating on the basis of the biblical notion that nature is to be conquered and destroyed.

Fahs finds this biblical dualism completely untenable. According to medicine and psychology, body and mind are one. Physicists and biochemists are finding that the boundaries between their fields are disappearing. The dividing line between the living and the non-living is no longer clear. Matter, once thought to be something to be touched and seen, is now believed to be energy at rest. Energy is found to be matter in excessive motion. Energy-matter is electrical. In every area of research we soon get to the intangible and the invisible which is nevertheless part of the material world. The universe as a whole may be alive. We can no longer set ourselves apart from the natural world because we are part of it. To deny the worth of the physical world is to deny our own worth. We live in one world—the cosmos as an interdependent unit.

Perhaps the most pervasive and destructive aspect of the biblical cosmology is the way in which the cosmos is seen to be controlled—by an almighty personal being who uses the forces of nature as a means of moral discipline. Even the concept of world community portrayed in the Bible is one of conquest and dominion—the good guys will win out over and destroy the bad guys and establish a kingdom of righteousness. Most of our society has not yet rejected the notion that life on earth is an unending battle between good and evil. We tend to feel that we must fight for causes that are good and against all that is wrong. We must fight for this reform. We must fight against this other party or group. We must even fight for peace. We divide the world into two camps, our friends and our enemies. Fahs points out that wherever a state of war exists, mutual respect vanishes.

The scientific conception of the universe is that it is self-governed and self-regulating, interrelated and interacting to the farthest reaches of space-time. Great powers of control lie within the very nature of existence in the ability of life to be active, to create, grow and evolve. The natural order resembles a democracy more than a kingdom, a balanced interdependence better described as cooperation. Unicellular living creatures first tried to cooperate and the existence of higher living forms is the result of this cooperation and specialization.

Does this concept of cooperation and interdependence mold the structures of our institutions, our buildings or the ways we relate to each other? Our schools, churches and patriarchal families reflect instead the old autocratic, hierarchical patterns of the biblical cosmology. Look for a moment at the way we build most of our churches and arrange our furniture. Steeples that reach up to heaven. Pulpits from which words are handed down from on high. Chairs that obediently face a raised altar that represents that all-powerful king in the sky. McLuhan has said that the medium is the message. As long as the words we hear and the spaces we live and worship in reflect an autocratic, warring and conquering world-view, we will continue to experience a deep split between our thoughts and feelings. To be healed we must break with the past and embrace the wonders of our own day.

The world-view Fahs developed as a result of her attempts to understand and integrate scientific knowledge can perhaps be expressed by the famous photograph of the earth taken from the moon. In 1952 Fahs wrote, "Scientists are developing a growing respect for all living things, and have discovered that cooperation with nature rather than ruling over it leads to humanity's larger good. We live in one world where not only are all people related but the total cosmos is one interdependent unit in which all the smaller units from human to animal, from vegetable to mineral, and on down to the tiniest particles of electrons and protons, mesons and photons in the cosmic rays, are of one kind. Altogether we are a unified cosmos."

Such a world-view constitutes a radical challenge to authoritarian patriarchal religion. On the occasion of her 100th birthday I wanted to make sure that the important theological contributions of this female theologian were not politely ignored.

Chapter 8

Feminism and Post-Modern Science

That same year, 1976, I completed my doctoral work in urban school psychology at Fordham University. I had been attending at night for about seven years while I worked as a school psychologist in public schools and then as a clinical psychologist in a psychiatric hospital. My goal had been to become licensed for private practice. After much deliberation, I decided to see if the Unitarian Universalist ministry might be a better place for me. I applied to and was accepted by Starr King School for the Ministry in Berkeley, California on the condition that I would study there for at least two years. I sold my little house in Florham Park, New Jersey, and in September packed up what would fit into our VW bus and set out for California. With me were my two daughters, Chris and Laura, my teen-age son Jim, and my son Scott who was home from college and helped drive. We dropped Jim off at college in Vermont. Our two cats stayed with a friend until they could make the trip to California by plane a few weeks later.

At Starr King I wasn't sure what courses to take. I had already taken most of the traditional courses years before at Drew. My advisor, Rev. Bob Kimball, president of the school, was very helpful, recommending courses in areas I had not studied. It was a question he asked me that caused my commitment to feminist spirituality to take shape and deepen. "Shirley," he said, "Where is your passion?"

Starr King is part of a consortium of nine theological schools—the Graduate Theological Union, and students can take courses in any of the nine schools. Three courses stand out in my memory, one on theologian Ernst Troelstch and one on science and religion at San Francisco Theological Seminary, and one on process theology at the Franciscan School. Process theology gave me a way to name my own developing theological position. The discoveries of

20th century science had led to a major paradigm shift or change in basic assumptions in the scientific community. It seemed to me that an analogous paradigm shift or change in basic assumptions was occurring in society generally as a result of the feminist movement. I published the following article in the *International Journal of Women's Studies*, suggesting that these paradigm shifts converge on the philosophical-theological issues of determinism, reductionism and the role of human imagination in research. Once again I sought out distinguished scholars who were writing about the relationship between science and religion, and distinguished feminist scholars who were leading the way in the feminist paradigm shift.

Elaine Morgan writes: It's just as hard for man to break the habit of thinking of himself as central to the species as it was to break the habit of thinking of himself as central to the universe. He sees himself quite unconsciously as the main line of evolution, with a female satellite revolving around him as the moon revolves around the earth. This not only causes him to overlook valuable clues to our ancestry, but sometimes leads him into making statements that are arrant and demonstrable nonsense.

Michael Polanyi writes: Scientific tradition derives its capacity for self-renewal from its belief in the presence of a hidden reality, of which current science is one aspect, while other aspects of it are to be revealed by future discoveries. Any tradition fostering the progress of thought must have this intention: to teach its current ideas as stages leading on to unknown truths which, when discovered, might dissent from the very teachings which engendered them.

In the scientific community a revolution has taken place which, according to scientists themselves, is of a magnitude similar to that caused by Newtonian physics. At the same time, women, by affirming their own experiences and perceptions in every area of life, are challenging the most basic assumptions of patriarchal society. The theological question to be considered here is how these paradigm shifts are related. Even to state the problem in that way implies a theological paradigm of my own. It can be stated simply: For me there is no secular world. Or as Pirsig puts it: "The Buddha, the Godhead, resides quite as comfortably in the circuits of a digital computer or the gears of a cycle transmission as (s)he does at the top of a mountain or in the petals of a flower. To think otherwise is to demean the Buddha—which is to demean oneself." There is only one real world and it includes all the complexities of distant galaxies, sub-atomic wave particles, organismic creativity and the human imagination.

The Scientific Paradigm Shift

At certain points in the history of science, discoveries are made which do not fit easily into the accepted paradigms. These discoveries do not simply add to scientific knowledge or change some peripheral details; they challenge some of its basic assumptions or ways of perceiving the world. Classic examples are Copernican astronomy and Newtonian physics. It is the contention of Kuhn and others (in Barbour 1966) that in the 20th century, the physical sciences made discoveries in several areas which amount to a revolution in the way scientists are being forced to view the world.

In the scientific world-view that prevailed in the modern era (as opposed to the post-modern) Newtonian mechanics formed the paradigm or ideal example of scientific work. According to Barbour, it supplied the guiding image of the kind of question that should be asked and type of concept that should be used. This view was deterministic in that nature was assumed to be a complete mechanical system of inflexible cause and effect governed by exact and absolute laws so that all future events are inexorably determined. It was reductionistic, believing that all phenomena would ultimately be explained by physical laws. Even human beings were viewed as complex machines. The title of a book by La Mettrie was *Man the Machine*. God was seen by some as the clock-maker who set the entire machine in motion and occasionally stepped in to adjust the mechanism, by others as a way to account for gaps in scientific knowledge, and by many as an unnecessary hypothesis.

Science was for a long time assumed to provide a literal description of an objective world, a view Barbour labels "naïve realism." A mind-body dualism was postulated. Mind and emotion as intangible and difficult to measure could be relegated to theology or philosophy.

Darwin's theory of evolution, appearing in the 19th century, might be considered the first large challenge to reigning world-views. It was perceived as just such a threat by religion because it appeared to undermine the exalted position of humans as distinct from animals, and because it suggested that the creation of species was a continuing process, still going on. Scientists, however, were not immediately bothered by the implications of such a process for the Newtonian paradigm. Evolution was seen as another indication of determinism.

Scientific discoveries of the 20th century undermined the world-view described above in a variety of ways. In physics especially the inadequacies of past assumptions began to be felt. Three major philosophical-theological issues or questions have re-emerged in the scientific paradigm shift: 1) *Critical Realism*—What is the role of human thought and imagination in furthering scientific knowledge? 2) *Reductionism*—Can all phenomena ultimately be explained by physical laws? 3) *Determinism*—Is the universe rigidly deterministic?

Critical Realism

One of the chief problems with the old paradigm was its failure to take seriously the role of creative imagination in advancing scientific knowledge. Objective empirical data were thought to be sufficient. Theories and models were always used but the importance of empirical data was seen as primary. Naïve realism assumed that everything in the physical world could be measured and pictured in a one-to-one correspondence with reality. When 20th century science began to deal with a subatomic world never directly observable, it became clearer that descriptions were often based upon hypothetical constructs and statistical probability, products of the human imagination, guided by experimental data but certainly not directly observable. For example, instead of the "planetary model" of electrons traveling in definite orbits around a nucleus, a complex wave-pattern throughout the region surrounding the nucleus had to be used to represent the atom. In general, observation of these variables, such as the position of an electron, is a matter of statistical probability. The wave pattern hypothesis permits the calculation of a probability distribution, not an exact value, for determining the position of the electron.

The place of theory in scientific research became a large and controversial question for philosophers of science. To what extent does a theory reflect objective reality and to what extent is it a product of the scientist's imagination? Barbour suggests that the most fruitful stance is one of critical realism. In naïve realism a one-to-one correspondence between the theory or model and reality is assumed. In critical realism a theory is held to reflect reality but not directly and not to the exclusion of the observer's imaginative contribution.

Reductionism

Another assumption of the earlier paradigm was reductionism, the assumption that the functioning of any system can be exhaustively explained in terms of the laws governing its component parts. But in quantum theory the atom must be represented as a whole rather than as a collection of parts; the system appears to be more than the totality of particles of which it is formed. Similarly in biology living organisms are integrated systems of dynamically inter-related parts; the parts have properties in relationship to the total organism which they do not have in isolation. Living organisms are also said to have emergent properties not predictable from the properties of their parts. Historically there have come into being new levels of reality with novel qualities not predictable from knowledge of the previous state of the world.

Determinism

The most strongly defended assumption of the old scientific paradigm is a thorough-going determinism. But in post-modern physics certain pairs of variables are related to each other in a very unusual way: the more accurately one of the quantities is known, the less accurately the other quantity is predictable. This is the principle of indeterminacy. The example used by Barbour is that the more accurately the position of an electron is measured in an experimental arrangement, the greater is the uncertainty in any prediction of its velocity.

The principle of indeterminacy suggested by post-modern physics can be seen as temporary human ignorance, in the belief that there are exact laws which will eventually be discovered. It can also be attributed to experimental or conceptual limitations, that is, uncertainty is introduced either by the process of observation or by the limits of the human conceptual capacity. There is the possibility, however, that indeterminacy really exists in nature, that there are real alternative potentialities in the atomic world.

Human freedom cannot be automatically extrapolated from the characteristics of subatomic physics. The experience of freedom, choice, decision-making may be determined by past events and conditionings or it may be that the influences of the past can be responded to in more than one way. Barbour suggests that insofar as human experience is an integrated event it displays a new type of unpredictability not derivative from atomic indeterminacy but from its own unitary organization at a higher level. The major point, however is that "physics can no longer be the chief witness called on behalf of reductionism or determinism."

Religion and the Scientific Paradigm Shift

The primary goal of science is understanding. Prediction and control are secondary, i.e. derived from that understanding. The relationship of science to religion is that the primary goal of religion is also understanding. Its moral and ethical positions and its view of the future (control and prediction?) are derived from that understanding. Should we then propose a hyphenated science-religion? The hyphen expresses my own paradigm and my understanding of it is traceable largely to the writings of Sophia Fahs. She was influenced by the findings of post-modern science and certainly it is easier to accept such a hyphen in the light of those findings. However, I believe an attempt was made in that direction by what Barbour describes as the Modernist movement in religion of the late 19th century and early 20th century. Barbour's description of the modernist viewpoint comes closest to the religious attitudes I remember hearing expressed by my parents and indeed the books he quotes were part of our collection. My impression is that Fahs too was heavily influenced by that point of view and that it is easier to enter the world of post-modern science from that paradigm than from the neo-orthodox or traditional ones. The reason for that ease lies in the fact that Darwin's theory of evolution dominated the modernist understanding of God and the world.

That understanding has been severely criticized because of some of the extrapolations made from the theory, notably the evolving moral grandeur of man (sic) which certainly failed to take seriously the lethal factor inherent in evolution. However, I feel that some very basic advances were made by the old modernists in our understanding of what constitutes religion in an age of science whether modern or post-modern. First, they made explicit the idea that science is a major source of our understanding of the universe and that as such its findings must be incorporated into theology. Second, they tried to eliminate the last vestiges of supernaturalism by proposing that God was immanent in the natural world and that transcendence or mystery was to be found not in a being or force outside that world but in the very evolutionary process *of* that world. Third, they deprived the Bible of its ultimate authority and superior status by viewing it as a human record, the story of one people's developing ideals and growing religious insights; this view opened the biblical religions not only to the findings of science but also to the insights of other world religions.

It seems to me that modernists in religion were caught up in the same paradigm as modern science. Although the theory of evolution can be seen as a challenge to a reductionist-determinist stance, it was at first seen by both science and religion as supporting that view. Science said, in effect, we are determined by our animal past and natural selection, i.e. the environment acting upon us, and there is nothing we can do about it. Religious modernists said, in effect, evolution produces change and we have evolved upward. There had to be an arbitrary faith in the ultimate goodness of this process to make such a religion possible. Such a faith, like any determinism, ignores present personal experience and may blunt any ethical imperative if the evolutionary process upward is seen as pre-determined.

Coming from a modernist paradigm into the theological world of neo-orthodoxy, I found Otto's "wholly other" too close to a return to the supernatural and Tillich's "ultimate reality" or "ground of being" much more acceptable. The newsreels of wartime atrocities I had watched every Saturday at the movies during World War II made me more than ready to abandon any naïve optimism about the goodness of evolution. I readily absorbed the existentialist emphasis upon direct experience. That theology turned to depth psychology to support a recognition of negative unconscious forces seemed quite natural to me. I wrestled with the problem of determinism in terms of sin and sickness and arrived at the agnostic view that based upon psychological knowledge at that time we simply did not know the answer. It seemed to me that neo-orthodoxy was dragging God and the biblical tradition in to fill the gap and would accept only that psychology which fitted into its structures.

It was not clear to me that, as Barbour points out, neo-orthodoxy or existentialist theology makes a sharp separation between the spheres of science and religion, claiming for religion the sphere of selfhood and personal experience and leaving the rest of the universe to science. It occurs to me that many physical scientists are able to accept religion on that basis; their attitude toward psychology is that it can never become a real, i.e. exact and observable, science anyway. In my four years at theological school in the 1950s nothing was said about any science except psychology—except in the writings of Sophia Fahs. Nevertheless the emphasis on personal experience as a source of religious knowledge seems to me to be a crucial ingredient for contemporary theology, and I see no reason why it has to depend upon such a separation of science and religion. Psychology is a science and its insights should be taken seriously. The death of supernaturalism means not only that science rather than a supernatural God must suggest our explanations; it also means that we must find meaning and value within this world. To do that we must have a broad understanding of science but we also have to become vividly aware of our personal and social situation. The significance of the post-modern paradigm shift lies not only in its challenge to reductionist and determinist philosophies (they may yet be proved correct) but in the sense of wonder and infinite mystery generated by the exploration of new depths and vastnesses in every science, including our knowledge of ourselves.

The Feminist Paradigm Shift

For women to become vividly aware of our personal situation we must undergo a paradigm shift of monumental proportions, one that makes the Copernican, Newtonian or post-modern scientific revolutions look like child's play. In terms of time periods alone the magnitude is overwhelming. We are attempting to change assumptions that have held sway not for two or three centuries but for two or three millennia. The assumptions are ingrained in us as well as in men which means that we must expend enormous energy just to break through those perceptions in ourselves. How then can it happen at all? And why is it happening now? I would suggest that the 18th and 19th century erosion of the biblical and popular image of God was necessary before women could even begin to free themselves. I think it is no accident that the first wave of feminism coincided with modernist evolutionary concepts of God and with the so-called pantheism of the transcendentalists. These models of God were impersonal and therefore less exclusively male. Evolution also suggested that change was possible although the full import of that was not immediately felt because of the determinist paradigm of modern science. There were more women ministers at the turn of the 20th century than there were in 1975. I also think it is no accident that such theologies were soon scorned and discredited by males who wished to re-establish the "otherness" and "sovereignty" and personal maleness of the patriarchal deity, and as that happened fewer and fewer women were drawn to the ministry.

The second wave of feminism coincided with the "death-of-God" theologies, which to the popular imagination meant the death of the patriarchal god. As the last vestiges of supernaturalism were removed, oppressed people had to find meaning and value in their immediate situations. Responsibility for our situation could no longer be left to a supernatural God. The findings of post-modern science suggest that responsibility also cannot be left to a deterministic universe. The rejection or retention of God-language today is not a matter of accepting or rejecting supernaturalism (although it may still be that for many people) but of choosing an appropriate label to describe the new sense of mystery, wonder and *responsibility* that arises from the findings of post-modern science. Religion may now be a matter of responsible self-affirmation or wholeness of being, part of which is a sense of participation in the ever-changing life of the universe.

Critical Realism

The critical realism of the post-modern scientist asserts that there are no uninterpreted facts, that all data are theory-laden. Models or analogies used to describe data are seen to reflect not only objective reality but also the imagination and point of view of the observer. Troeltsch arrived at a similar conclusion regarding the writing of history, that the historian's account is inevitably distorted by *his* own cultural and personal biases. I have used the masculine pronoun deliberately. Women are pointing out that all of our history, all of our science, all of our literature, all of our art, all of our religions, all of our philosophy, all of our governments, all of our justice, all of our goals, the very language we speak, have been written, designed and constructed by and for the benefit of males. We are suggesting that the masculine description of reality is only partially accurate because it ignores the experience of half of the human race and because, like every description, it is inevitably colored by the point of view of the observer. Female scholars in every field are beginning to check the data using female imagination and models. They are finding (to use Barbour's criteria) that the male "facts" do not always fit in with the empirical data of female observation; that there are large gaps and inconsistencies which can often be overcome by introducing a female viewpoint; and that male models are not readily extensible to female experience. Elaine Morgan's popular anthropological work *The Descent of Woman* is an excellent and amusing example of this process. Consider one brief passage. Speaking of the prehominid ape who, she suggests, has taken to the seashore during the Pliocene drought, Morgan writes:

> "She switched easily, almost without noticing it, from eating small scuttling insects to eating small scuttling shrimps and baby crabs . . . Besides the shrimps there were larger creatures with harder shells, resembling mussels and oysters and lobsters. Her mate used to crunch through the shells or pry them open with his dagger-like canines; she was envious of this because being daggerless she couldn't manage it. One idle afternoon after a good deal of trial and error she picked up a pebble—this required no luck at all because the beach was covered with thousands of pebbles—and hit one of the shells with it, and the shell cracked. She tried it again, and it worked every time. So

she became a tool user, and the male watched her and imitated her."

The task however is far more frightening than such an academic description suggests. The most basic change, as Daly points out, has to take place in women, in our being and self-image. As women we have been alienated from our own deepest identity and have received a certain security in return for accepting very limited identities. Such roles have been our only security and source of community. Breaking out of these roles requires a realization that there is an existential conflict between the self and structures that have given such crippling security. The sad truth is that many strong women are worn out in the struggle to break out of these limits before reaching the higher levels of creativity. One faces a sea of anxieties including the loss of social approval, guilt over refusing to do what society demands, and an overwhelming sense of meaninglessness when the old meanings, role definitions and life expectations are rejected and "one emerges into a world *without models.*"

Daly has said that "It is necessary to grasp the fundamental fact that women have had the power of *naming* stolen from us. We have not been free to use our own power to name ourselves, the world, or God." The models, the names, the languages imposed by men have been false not only because they are partial, but because they function to prevent human becoming in women. For example, Daly points out that Jesus as a model, a revelatory event or incarnation is not only a one-sided image that functions to glorify maleness. He also represents the imagery of the scapegoat or sacrificial victim. The image inspires guilt which is transferred to the Other who is then cast in the role of scapegoat. (This process has been amply documented not only by clinical case studies in psychology but by a wealth of experimental data on the authoritarian personality.) As Daly makes clear, women have been the primary scapegoats, urged to follow the model of sacrificial love, but denied the dignity of this role by being excluded from the priesthood and identified with Eve and evil.

But where are we to look for alternative models? Women have been wiped out of history. There has been a failure to record the creative activity of great and talented women under patriarchy. There has also been a failure to recognize the increasing evidence that there was a matrifocal world before the era of patriarchy. In biology the fact that initially all mammalian embryos are females has been quietly ignored. Any data that would threaten patriarchal assumptions has been ignored or trivialized. Daly suggests that there are inherent difficulties in looking to any person as a model because it is usually necessary to shrink the self in order to imitate a model. The validity of a model lies in its ability to spark self-affirmation in another person, to function as a model breaker pointing beyond present limitations to future potential.

It is difficult, however, to express the full extent of the anxiety and confusion involved in affirming one's selfhood and experience without the aid of acceptable models. At age 13, I read a biography of Marie Curie. At some level I suppose she has functioned as a model, a strong woman who achieved great heights in science without denying herself the satisfactions of a family. But for many years her image was forgotten because I was convinced that she was, after all, a genius, an exception, not a realistic model for me. Even when a constructive model is identified, one that would encourage the growth of selfhood, the force of patriarchal socialization operates to discount it. So pressing is the need for a religious model that the Virgin Mary is perceived by some feminists as a manifestation of the ancient Great Goddess.

Reductionism

Women as defined by patriarchy are living examples of reductionist philosophy in its most destructive form. A woman's whole self is defined by men in terms of her sexuality. The false identities she is forced to assume are based upon defining her totality in terms of her reproductive parts. Theologian Helmut Thielicke writes: "It is, so to speak, the vocation of the woman to be lover, companion, and mother. And even the unmarried woman fulfills her calling in accord with the essential image of herself only when these fundamental characteristics, which are designed for wifehood and motherhood, undergo a sublimating transformation, but still remain discernible . . ."

This is, I think, a fine example of the "arrant and demonstrable nonsense" mentioned by Morgan. On the scientific front Freudian theory describes woman's personality in terms of penis-envy. Men of course can sublimate their sexual energies in a vast array of activities but for women the only fulfillment is said to be motherhood. Our socialization into a stereotyped sex role has allowed us to believe that this reduction of self was natural. As Daly points out, "Mothers in our culture are cajoled into killing off the self-actualization of their daughters and daughters learn to hate them for it." In a sexist society where all the symbols, models and conceptual formulations are male creations which do not reflect female experience, we tend to adopt a false self-image. When that happens we simply do not see the situation. We ask only the questions allowed within the sexist thought structures. We learn to ignore all the rest of our experience, classifying it automatically as unimportant or meaningless. We become the stereotype and that partial becoming reinforces the apparent reality of the stereotype. It seems to me that the female stereotype and perhaps all stereotypes are based upon a reductionist stance. Our reduction to sex objects is the reason the so-called sexual revolution does not liberate us. As Daly comments, the sexual freedom that recently has been forced upon women leaves no freedom to refuse to be defined by sex. She suggests that the draining of women's energies by obsession with sexuality is another form of rape, "a rape of mind and will that robs the female self of precious time, energy and self-esteem."

There are at least three obvious implications of a non-reductionist view of women: 1) We need not define ourselves in terms of sex alone; 2) We need not deny our sexual selves in order to explore our intellectual and religious selves; 3) Our wholeness as persons will be the integration of a wide range of potentialities.

Determinism

Becoming, with or without models, implies a stance in regard to determinism. Even modernist evolutionary determinism assumed that the directions already taken by an evolving universe were pre-determined and therefore right and good. For women this meant not only that biology was destiny but that the social structures that had evolved were also destiny. Daly points out "we have no power *over* the ultimately real, and whatever authentic power we have is derived from participation in ultimate reality." It makes a difference whether that reality is perceived as rigidly determined, or as containing a range of possibilities. I am reminded of the extensive controversies in psychology concerning the measurement of intelligence. Is it a fixed quantity genetically determined or the result of environmental influences upon the infant and young child? The widely accepted view today, based upon vast quantities of data, is that intelligence is not fixed at a certain numerical point; that genetics determines a particular range of potentiality, a range which in most cases cuts across the arbitrary boundaries of retardation and normality; that the amount of development of that potential depends upon the environment. This example seems to me to be analogous to (though not derived from) the indeterminacy found in other sciences. As women we can assume that personally and socially there has always existed a range of possibilities, and most importantly that such a range exists for the future. Daly suggests that the process of becoming as it is emerging in women potentially includes both the individualistic dimension of depth, and revolutionary participation in history because it strikes at both the internalized images and the externalized structures of patriarchy. "In the very process of becoming actual persons, of confronting the non-being of our situation, women are bearers of history . . . what is at stake is a real leap in human evolution, initiated by women."

Morgan who thinks in evolutionary chunks of time, agrees with Daly that women have before them some cosmic possibilities as the bearers of history, the initiators of an evolutionary leap. Her rationale, however, is a bit more earthy than Daly's. She suggests that with the advent of the pill, "woman is beginning to get her finger on the genetic trigger" and the process of husband-selecting might for the first time begin to have some genetic significance. She writes: "It may be that for Homo Sapiens in the future, extreme manifestations of the behavior patterns of dominance and aggression will be evolutionarily at a discount; and if that happens he will begin to shed them as once, long ago, he shed his coat of fur."

Looking Ahead

We need to keep in mind the fact that neither paradigm shift is complete. Many scientists still espouse a determinist-reductionist view of reality and most men and many women still espouse a determinist-reductionist view of women. The role of the human imagination and the limits of objectivity are still not given adequate recognition. Instrumentalists who perceive models merely as useful fictions whose truth or falsity is irrelevant are perhaps more numerous than critical realists. It is my impression that such scientists tend to see the primary goal of science as prediction and control rather than as understanding for its own sake. This attitude is particularly evident in our propensity for applying technology without an adequate understanding of the complex interconnectedness of nature with resulting environmental problems. Authentic science like authentic selfhood depends upon participation in the ultimate reality of the universe. A paradigm or set of assumptions is not abandoned because it is proved to be false but because new discoveries in reality require a more complete explanation. The new paradigm not only is more adequate in dealing with new discoveries; it is also able to suggest reasons for the partial validity of the old paradigm. A recurrent theme in feminism is the awareness that the liberation of women ultimately implies a liberation of men because the sex role stereotypes have stunted certain kinds of development in men. Men do not typically show the characteristics they project onto the Other. But it is just this ability of the patriarchal mind to think in terms of sharp dichotomies that made possible the distinction between subject and object so useful in the development of modern science. The usefulness of that kind of analysis is not negated by post-modern science. It is found to be necessary but partial in terms of understanding the universe.

I would suggest that the new paradigm in science does negate or falsify the old to the extent: 1) that partial understanding is assumed to be total, and 2) that the assumptions of the old prevent rather than encourage the questioning of its parameters. Similarly, feminism negates or falsifies the patriarchal paradigm to the extent that: 1) male understanding is equated with human understanding, and 2) patriarchal assumptions prevent rather than encourage questioning of its structures. To put it another way, what women want is not patriarchy spelled with an *m* but a whole new way of life in which male understanding and female understanding are integrated and there is an openness to new questions and possibilities.

Chapter 9

Feminist Thealogy as a New Religion

If the divine could be considered the shape of growth and creativity in all of life, as process theology seemed to suggest, it occurred to me that with the insights of feminist thealogy a new religion might be emerging.

When the first picture of the earth taken from the moon appeared on the front page of the New York Times I felt that it was a religious event of profound significance. The Times, quite appropriately, had asked poet Archibald MacLeish to write the accompanying article. Here it was at last, the longed-for symbol of a world-view as new as the space age yet as old as the earth itself. What religion, I wondered, would recognize the psychological, sociological and cosmological potential in that contemporary symbol? Who would lift it up and articulate the religious world-view of the future?

Years ago when I attended a gathering of women who worship the Goddess, and later when I participated in an international conference of Unitarian Universalist women, there it was, that photo of the earth taken from the moon, centrally and prominently displayed. Symbol of Mother Earth? Yes, but for sophisticated modern women (and men) much more: wholeness of body and spirit, oneness of humanity, and our interconnectedness with the natural world. Not all feminists identify themselves as Goddess worshippers, but among a growing number of women who value the religious or creative dimension in life, there may be a new religion in the making. Let us examine several aspects of that religion to see what it may have to offer as the world-view of the future.

In recent years, many women have been saying that the Great Goddess is re-emerging. That statement appears to have several meanings. The first is that women have rediscovered the Goddess within and are asserting themselves in the expression of their full human potential. In this sense the Goddess represents the striving of modern women to claim their own power and to break out of the stereotyped roles to which they have been confined in patriarchal societies. A second meaning of the re-emergence of the Goddess is that through the findings of modern archeology women have been researching their pre-patriarchal roots and discovering that female images of divine power pervaded the entire ancient world. This research allows women to connect with what the Great Goddess meant to human beings in prehistoric and early historic times. It grounds us all in a religious history which spanned thousands of years and was based upon female creativity and life stages, a history we are attempting to integrate into our modern lives.

Goddess religion has two further meanings which may have universal power and validity. She reminds us that we are all born of woman and of the earth. Our first human relationship is with woman as mother and our first knowledge of what it is to be human is gathered there. Patriarchal society has held that that primary relationship must be radically rejected and left behind in order for us to become adults. As a result women, particularly mothers, have been devalued and blamed for every illness of society. We have been carefully taught to hate not only ourselves as women but other groups as well. The return of the Goddess suggests that humanity is one and that we need to reclaim and integrate the nurturing mother in all of us before our hatred destroys us.

The other universal meaning of the Goddess today is as a symbol of the life-supporting delicate ecological balance of the earth. Here the Goddess symbol connects with the contemporary ecological concerns of both women and men, and here is where the photo of the earth taken from the moon speaks with particular power to all of us. Environmentalist Theodore Roszak has made the poetic suggestion that we consider the earth as a whole to be a sentient being, a Goddess of whom we are a part, a Goddess who may be moving to stop the destruction of her life-giving systems by creating ecologically concerned humans.

The rituals and celebrations of the Goddess religion seem to focus on these two universal themes: the life stages of woman and the beauty and wonder of the natural world. The ancient Goddess often appeared in three aspects—the youthful maiden, the mother, and the wise crone. These phases and the difficult transition from one to another are being celebrated by modern women. An interesting development here is the contemporary importance given to the crone, not as a parent to be obeyed or rejected, but as a friend who is lovingly consulted because her wisdom is valued. At a time when our senior citizens are trying to claim their rightful place in our society, such validation of age and wisdom meets an urgent religious need. Woman in all her life stages celebrates her strength in relation to the cycles of nature, the most obvious connection being between menses and the waxing and waning moon. Celebrations are held regularly at the time of the full moon. The changing seasons are also celebrated, and an attempt is made to be in touch with and to relate one's life to the rhythms of nature. The natural world is viewed with wonder, and reverence is expressed for all forms of life. Contemporary feminists seem to affirm a kind of human wisdom which is grounded in the reality of the natural world. The timeliness of such wisdom in view of our ecological crisis is obvious.

Many years ago theologian Ernst Troeltsch ended his voluminous history of the social teachings of Christianity with the comment that for modern people "the kingdom of God is within." He concluded that the only type of religion possible in the modern world was the "mystic" type. By that he meant a religion in which each individual was responsible for her own life and beliefs. The conclusion saddened him because he felt that such a religion could never appeal to large numbers of people; what was needed was a new completion or world-view through which such inner individual religion could be expressed in the world. He wrote: ". . . then here new thoughts will be necessary which have not yet been thought, and which correspond to this situation as the older forms have corresponded to older situations . . . Today, in the midst of a completely new cultural situation, the old completions have become impossible. A new completion is thus necessary."

Some sixty years later feminist theologian Mary Daly seemed to be announcing such a new completion (though not for Christianity as Troeltsch would have hoped) when she wrote: "In a real sense the symbols of patriarchal religion deserved to 'die.' What women's becoming can mean is something beyond their death and beyond their rebirth . . . Rather, women's becoming is something more like a new creation."

Feminist scholar Barbara G. Walker writes, "Thealogy is both new and old: a new view of Woman, her spirituality, and her achievements, plus a much-needed return to her roots. Underneath the surface of our patriarchal society, there are female voices calling out for this—more and more of them each year . . . Suppose we were free to recognize deity for what it really is, an archetypal symbol in some sense evolved by the mind of every individual born of woman: a human phenomenon only, but an important and powerful one. That would be thealogy, and it would be new. And it would lead us back to the Mother."

I would suggest that the symbols for a contemporary and future religious world-view are already at hand in the re-emergence of the Goddess and in that photo of the earth taken from the moon, and that feminist spirituality could very well articulate the religion of the future.

Chapter 10

Our Sacred History as Women

Starr King provided me an opportunity to research in some depth the roots of women's religious history in pre-historic and early historic times when the divine was almost universally imaged as female. It is difficult to convey in words the excitement that some of us women theological students felt as our own religious heritage began to be unearthed. Rev. Emily Champagne who had graduated from Starr King in the sixties returned to do some research. She discovered Enheduanna, a real high priestess, poet and thealogian who lived in the ancient Sumerian city of Ur about 2360 BCE and wrote a series of hymns to the Goddess Inanna. Why, we wondered, had we heard nothing about her in our regular classes?

My dear friend Chris Bailey came running in from the library one day exclaiming, "Look, look what I found!" She held up a recording. Archeologists had found Sumerian clay tablets with unusual markings as well as words. They figured out that it was musical notation. The words were a hymn to the moon goddess. They constructed a lyre typical of the time and played and sang the hymn for the recording. Listening to that music, preserved for us across more than three millennia, was a sacred moment.

Our sacred history as women is a story grounded in the findings of 20th century archeology and anthropology. At the same time it is a story that transcends those findings as it serves a mythic function in our lives. Great myths reflect and teach us many truths about ourselves, our history and our society. Divine power, the power of life and death, was for many thousands of years thought to be female.

Archeologists such as Raphael Patai, Rachel Levy and Marija Gimbutas tell us that for many thousands of years human beings worshipped this divine mother. In Joseph Campbell's opinion, "There can be no doubt that in the very earliest ages of human history, the magical force and wonder of the female was no less a marvel than the universe itself and this gave to women a prodigious power."

Myths tell us that in very early times the Goddess reigned. If the myths of a culture reflect its social arrangements, women must have had power and respect. In later times myths tell us that male deities waged battles against the Goddess, tricked her into giving up her power or, if she was very powerful, married her. If the myths of a culture reflect its social arrangements, women must have suffered an overall loss of power and respect. And yet, in the old pagan religions, even after all the battles and the exalting of the male deities to the most powerful positions, the Goddesses were still there. Zeus had to ask Themis to convene the deities. Hera married Zeus, but fought him all the way. And it was Athena who stood in the Parthenon.

Over the course of millennia the Great Goddess was worshipped in three separate aspects: as the maiden, the mother, and the crone. The three aspects of the Goddess were linked to the phases of the moon—the waxing moon was the maiden with all her possibilities, the full moon was the abundance of the mother, and the waning moon was the wisdom of the old woman. Women felt in their own bodies and menstrual cycles a very close connection with the phases of the moon and the cycles of birth, growth and death that they saw in the plants and animals around them.

Women were thought to be endowed with divine power because they could bleed without harm, give birth to new life and provide milk. Menstrual blood was sacred and thought to contain the divine wisdom that created new human beings. People believed that when a woman stopped bleeding she was storing and retaining that divine wisdom.

Another way of describing the triple Goddess was as Creator, Preserver and Destroyer. In this rendition the Crone takes on not only the wisdom but also the power of death. She is the one who knows when an individual life must end in order for new life to begin. She is the Goddess of that mysterious transformation that occurs as we are returned to the earth, to the ongoing cycle of life and death. In the old Goddess religions death was believed to be part of the cycle of life. When the male gods sought to control or take over the powers of the old goddesses, it was the Crone, the Destroyer they feared and hated most.

The male consort of the Goddess gradually became more and more important and powerful. Mythology tells us that in early historic times Goddesses and Gods reigned together with varying amounts of power. Eventually the male deities became the chief deities. In Judaism and Christianity the male God became the only deity.

In regard to Judaism and Christianity I discovered that some feminists insist that male scholars and clergy down through the centuries have misinterpreted and distorted the message of the biblical tradition which proclaims justice and love for all persons, male and female. The God of the Bible had a female partner for many centuries and was at times described with female imagery; there were female prophets and judges; Jesus treated women with the same dignity that he did men; in the early Christian church women preached and taught and shared all responsibilities equally with men; and Paul at his best proclaimed that "in Christ there is neither male nor female." In later centuries Jesus' mother Mary became an exalted female presence in Christianity. Church history was being re-examined to discover the contributions of strong women, and the writings of female mystics were being read with new interest.

One of the most interesting mid-century discoveries was a large collection of ancient manuscripts buried in Upper Egypt by early Christians. These writings included a number of gospels, versions of Jesus' life and work written by very early Gnostic Christians and never before available to us. Scholar Elaine Pagels who analyzed a large number of these writings, pointed out that Gnostic Christians used many female images to refer to the divine, and that women had far more power and responsibility in Gnostic churches than in those that became orthodox. It is interesting too that Mary Magdalene was considered a person of power and influence, perhaps even an apostle, among the Gnostic Christians. Another phenomenon of interest to women is that the organization of Gnostic churches appears to have been nonhierarchical and non-authoritarian. These ancient texts give strong support to the notion that the suppression of women in the Christian Church as we have known it occurred for political reasons and is a distortion of Christianity as it was known in the early churches.

If we accept the theory that myths reflect the power structures of societies, it follows that women had significant power in the early history of humanity but had that power wrested away in a long struggle.

The big question, of course, was why? Why did dominating men need to gain control and why did women allow it to happen? At first there were only three basic theories that had been suggested to explain this shift in power.

The first was that of nineteenth century scholars Johann Jakob Bachofen and others. They were struck by the strong presence of women in ancient mythologies and suggested that human society had evolved through two stages before it became patriarchal. The first stage was a time of sexual promiscuity and disorder. When that stage became intolerable, the mothers established a matriarchal rule in order to protect and provide for the children. Men were treated as inferior, and their only access to power was through their sisters. When this system became intolerable, the men overthrew the matriarchy and established male rule. Patriarchy was considered to be a higher form of society. It did not occur to them that it, too, might become intolerable. Later anthropologists and archeologists have not found evidence of early matriarchy if it is defined as the reverse of patriarchy, nor a stage of "sexual promiscuity and disorder." Evidence does not support the domination of men by women. It does, however, support the presence of cultures with matrilineal descent and power shared more equally between men and women than is the case in the later patriarchal societies.

The second theory to explain the shift in power is based on Jungian psychology. Psychoanalyst Carl Jung took seriously the ancient mythologies as a source for understanding human psychology. He too noted the powerful presence of women in the old myths. Jung's theory makes an analogy between individual development and societal development. An individual is completely nurtured and cared for by her or his mother early in life. Later, in order to grow, she or he must grow out of infant bliss and go into the father's world. The assumption, of course, is that the adult world is a male one. Similarly, according to Jung, the human species first revered only female power; later it had to separate itself from female deities and turn to male gods. Again, the shift from female to male identification is seen as an evolution to a higher form of religion and society, with little awareness that a shift to patriarchy may be regressive or that the future may demand further change.

Feminist scholar Merlin Stone offered a third theory. She traced the known and hypothesized migrations of early people and suggested that waves of Indo-Europeans surged southward and conquered and merged with the inhabitants of the ancient Near East and the Mediterranean region. These Indo-Europeans were nomadic herders, unlike the settled agricultural peoples they conquered. Their chief gods were male and their society was patriarchal, whereas the agricultural peoples revered nature goddesses and had matrifocal societies. When the Indo-Europeans conquered the locals, the myths of the two cultures merged, but the conquering male gods eventually gained prominence. Archeologist Marija Gimbutas later advanced a similar theory.

In the years since then several more interesting theories have been suggested. Scholar Riane Eisler and many geneticists agree with Stone and Gimbutas that it was the successive migrations of patriarchal Indo-Europeans into Old Europe and the Mediterranean area which caused the shift in divine and societal power. Eisler goes on to present evidence from many sources that pre-patriarchal cultures were indeed not matriarchal but were organized on a partnership basis where women as well as men were held in high esteem within the community and held many positions of power. Her thesis is that the shift was not from matriarchal to patriarchal but from partnership, or shared power, to patriarchal domination.

Leonard Shlain, a brain surgeon, suggests that it was the development of writing, specifically the very abstract alphabet, and the increased importance of the left brain that caused women to lose their earlier power. His thesis is that in prehistoric times, before writing, the right brain, the side that deals mainly in images and the ability to perceive the totality of a scene, was dominant for survival and women excelled. When the linear and abstract abilities of the left brain became more necessary, men excelled and became dominant. According to Shlain, in every culture literacy is accompanied by the rise of patriarchy.

Feminist writer Carol Lee Flinders offers yet another theory. She contrasts what she labels the early values of Belonging with the later values of Enterprise. Her thesis, based upon her study of extensive anthropological research, suggests that the very ancient hunter-gatherers needed a strong and egalitarian sense of belonging in order to survive. Everyone was dependent upon the shared knowledge and care of the whole group. Groups were small, everyone knew everyone, and if conflicts arose they were handled quietly or with humor because conflict was a threat to survival. Flinders suggests that it was the development of agriculture, the owning and defending of land, that gradually allowed men to become more and more violent and the old values of belonging and caring to be gradually delegated exclusively to women. The new values of Enterprise, which included great inventiveness, but also dominance and control, became the province of men. She suggests that human beings could have integrated the positive aspects of Enterprise and of Belonging in much better ways than they have, and must do so in the future.

History is an ever-changing field, and these are only some of the current theories. New research is emerging daily from both female and male historians. The important fact here for me was that women lost power in the ancient Western world, and that women's power needed to be reclaimed in creative ways in today's world.

In the nineteen seventies, at the Graduate Theological Union the Office of Women's Affairs sponsored a discussion group which I participated in during my years at Starr King. One of our concerns was how to get women's lost sacred history into the curriculum of the theological schools. We had occasional guest speakers, or one session of a full year course might be about women, but most of our theological education was like the work of Ernst Troelstch. He wrote volumes and never mentioned women at all except in an occasional footnote.

During that time I attended a large Goddess conference at the University of California in Santa Cruz. There I first experienced a pagan ritual led by Z. Budapest and heard feminist thea/ologian Carol Christ speak about "Why Women Need the Goddess." When I returned to my typing job in one of the GTU offices, Jacob Needleman stopped by one day to tell us about a large grant he had received to study new religious movements in America. He said he had distributed some of the money to students who were interviewing and writing about various gurus. I asked him if anyone was studying the Goddess religion that was becoming popular among many women. He said no, and asked me to tell him about it. I told him about the conference. He said that if I would write a paper and teach a course at GTU about the Goddess religion he could offer me a grant of $1000. I accepted the offer with great excitement and about a dozen women students registered for the course. Still, we wondered if the study of women's religious history would ever be a permanent part of theological education. Some thirty years later the GTU announced a whole new program: Women's Studies in Religion. When my daughter Laura saw the brochure on my desk, she said, "That's new?"

Chapter 11
Revolution by Resolution

As a woman planning to become a minister, it was clear to me that a woman who stepped up to the pulpit had already made a powerful thea/ological statement before she said a word. Her very presence shattered the deeply ingrained assumptions of Western traditions whether theist or humanist. When Elizabeth Cady Stanton and her friends were planning the Women's Rights Convention in 1848 they deliberated seriously about whether or not they should speak before an audience. They thought perhaps they should ask a man to speak for them. A woman in the pulpit every Sunday was unthinkable. But the women dared to speak and other women dared to imagine being in the pulpit. By 1870 there were five female clergy. By 1890 the Universalists and the Unitarians together had ordained about 70 women. And by the turn of the 20th century there were 101. Unfortunately we then lost our foothold in the ministry. By 1975 there were only 41 ordained women in our ministry, and the presence of a woman in the pulpit was a very rare event.

Many Unitarian Universalist women were leaders in the feminist movement of the late sixties and early seventies, and it was inevitable that we would bring feminism into our congregations. We faced quite a task. Because we draw on many traditions, we felt we had to challenge all the major world religions as patriarchal and sexist. We looked at our own hymnal and our principles and purposes and said, "That language has to go!" The humanist men in our congregations used to go through the old hymnal and change the word *God* to *man*. Somehow this didn't help us women very much.

As a result of the efforts of many women our General Assembly unanimously passed a Women and Religion Resolution in 1977. It demanded that we, as a religious people professing the inherent worth and dignity of every person, examine our theologies, our language and our organizational structures so as to root out sexism in every area of our religious life.

A continental Women and Religion Committee was formed and similar committees were organized in each of our districts to implement the resolution. I was in Berkeley, California at Starr King School at the time and I became involved in the work of the district Women & Religion Task Force. It was an exciting time as we planned women's retreats and encouraged each other to challenge the sexist language in worship and to claim our own voices and power. Women were writing new songs and hymns and sermons.

There was also a woman, Rev. Leslie Westbrook, on the staff at our headquarters in Boston; her job was to find ways to implement the resolution. As a direct result of her work, an affirmative action program was developed to encourage more women to enter our ministry, and a sexism audit was devised so that our denominational staff and our congregations could examine their organizations for sexism. Several continent-wide conferences also were held on the subject of women and religion.

In the years since then hundreds of women have been ordained. Even before the Women & Religion resolution was passed, the women ministers had formed a new organization—the Ministerial Sisterhood-Unitarian Universalist or MS-UU. They felt a need to have such an organization to advocate for themselves as they faced the lingering sexist attitudes of some of their male colleagues and some of our congregations.

I was ordained myself in 1980 by the Northern Hills Fellowship in Cincinnati, Ohio. Northern Hills was looking for their first minister, they had an attractive building and they had raised enough money to pay a full time minister for two years. Their hope was that in two years they would grow enough to continue paying the minister. An experienced minister probably would have known better than to take the job. But I was new to the profession and I liked the people so I accepted their call. Of course we didn't grow enough, so I left after two and a half years. I suggested that they get an extension minister, not only trained in growth but partly paid by the Unitarian Universalist Association. They did so and have been able to support a full time minister ever since.

As for me, I was torn. I loved being a minister, but I thought maybe I was responsible for our failure to grow. I wondered if perhaps I should have stayed in psychology. I had always considered my work in psychology a kind of ministry anyway. I decided to return to my former profession and complete my earlier goal of becoming licensed for private practice. I stayed in Cincinnati where I found two part time positions—one as a psychologist at the University of Cincinnati Counseling Center and another as a therapist for the Catholic Archdiocese counseling center for priests and nuns.

I was surprised that the Catholic counseling center hired me, a Unitarian Universalist minister, to be one of their therapists. My agreement with those in charge was that I would say nothing about my own background to clients unless asked directly. I found the nuns I worked with to be some of the most interesting and thoughtful clients I ever had. They were used to introspection and were able to use therapy effectively in their lives. Interesting also was the fact that each one, after a few sessions looked at me with kind questioning eyes and said, "You're not Catholic are you?" They couldn't seem to say how they knew, except for one woman who thought maybe it was because I seemed not to have much sense of guilt. Well, I do think there is both healthy guilt—feeling truly sorry when something one says or does has hurt another person—and unhealthy guilt where one feels guilty just about being oneself. Perhaps my client had correctly zeroed in on our UU theological rejection of original sin.

I also enrolled in a year-long Gestalt Training Program. Then I took the psychology licensing exam as a California candidate, passed it, and returned to California where both of my daughters were living. There I connected with a private practice group in the San Diego area. I stayed there for four years.

Because it takes awhile to build a private practice, I also worked part time at the county jail for women. At that time it was the only county jail (as distinct from a state prison) in the country which had a psychiatric program. I mention it here because my work there enabled me to encounter a level of society I had never known previously. Our team had a psychiatrist, a clinical psychologist (me), a social worker, an occupational therapist and a mental health specialist. We met with the women individually and in small groups to see if there were ways that they could be helped. Jails have an interesting combination of people. Some are serving short sentences for stealing or prostitution while others are awaiting trials for drug dealing or murder.

The women came mostly from a world in which breaking the law was irrelevant. Their goal in life was simply survival. We couldn't seem to convince them that breaking a law was important. Some even considered jail a sort of resting place where they had a bed, meals, and a place to take a shower. Some regaled us with stories of easily lifting toys from department stores and selling them on the street. But when they quietly painted facial masks in the group, the depth of anger and depression they revealed was overwhelming. Reading their case histories it was clear that most of the women were born into such violence and neglect as we professionals could barely imagine. In that light their survival at all seemed amazing. Whatever choices, if any, they might have had in their lives, they were not the same kinds of choices I had had. I doubt if our work at the jail helped them much, given their histories and their realistic but sadly limited goal of survival. The women's jail was quite a distance from the city. When a woman was released she was simply given bus fare back to the city. I still think of those women. They greatly enlarged my view of what justice—or psychology—is really about, especially for women.

In the late eighties MS-UU held a meeting in Santa Barbara. I decided to attend. There we learned that the Unitarian Universalist Ministers Association of which we were all members proposed an all-male slate of officers to be elected at our annual meeting. MS-UU was able to speak on behalf of the women ministers and to suggest women for some of the offices. Some women were indeed elected. I enjoyed being with my colleagues and I felt once again the old excitement about being a minister. I began a search process and the following year was called to serve the UU Fellowship of Mobile, Alabama three quarter time, and the UU Church in Jackson, Mississippi one quarter time. We women ministers kept in touch through *Gleanings*, the MS-UU newsletter. Rev. Marjorie Leaming was the editor for many years. I took on that job after she retired. I enjoyed gathering news and articles from the women and writing a little column for each issue. In the nineties one of our projects was to provide encouragement and some financial support for our ministerial sisters in Transylvania. With our help they were able to gather for small conferences to support each other.

As the years went by and more and more women were ordained there seemed to be less need for a separate ministerial organization for women. And so in 2005 we ended the organization. I wonder if women will once again lose our foothold in the ministry as we did in the early 20th century. Or will we perhaps take over the profession of ministry only to see it lose status in what continues to be largely a patriarchal society? My hope is that a new generation of women will feel empowered by our work to assert themselves in whatever way is needed in the future.

Over the years our hymnal and our principles and purposes document have been transformed with inclusive language; we now ordain ministers of religious education, a traditionally non-ordained female preserve; and we recognize community ministries which are also often chosen by women. Women have taken on top leadership positions at our headquarters and in our congregations. We have created new ceremonies such as the sharing of joys and concerns as part of our worship and more and more often we arrange our furniture in non-hierarchical patterns.

These very significant practical changes, however, are not the whole story. They are the outward and visible signs of an inner and less visible transformation. As another way of implementing the Women and Religion Resolution, I was asked by Rev. Westbrook to devise a course of study on feminist theology. It was an opportunity to bring the chambers of feminist spirituality into interaction with some of the chambers of Unitarian Universalism. In preparation for writing such a course, I attended the UU Women & Religion Convocation held in East Lansing, Michigan in 1980. Feminist thealogy scholars Carol Christ and Naomi Goldenberg whose writings I already admired were featured speakers. It was a continent-wide gathering where, besides hearing speakers, women created interesting new worship experiences. The most memorable was one in which women leaders brought small amounts of water from waterways near their homes—oceans, lakes and rivers—and poured them into a huge bowl, mentioning each by name. The symbolism was dramatic. Women from all of these places and more came to find our own religious heritage and to share our spiritual journeys as women.

The course that eventually emerged is called *Cakes for the Queen of Heaven*. Now where did I get such a title? From the Bible! I found two extraordinary passages in the Book of Jeremiah. In the first one God is speaking to Jeremiah saying: "Do you not see what they do in the cities of Judah and in the streets of Jerusalem? The children gather wood and the fathers kindle the fire and the women knead the dough to make cakes to the Queen of Heaven, and they pour out libations to other gods, in order to anger me!" (RSV 7:17-18)

Jeremiah warns the people that if they do not stop worshipping the Queen of Heaven and turn only to Yahweh, a great catastrophe will occur. Later, after there is a great catastrophe and they are exiled in Egypt, Jeremiah tells the people it happened because they continued to worship the Queen of Heaven. But the people talk back to the prophet and they say: "As for the word that you have spoken to us in the name of Yahweh—we shall not listen to you. But we shall without fail do everything as we said: we shall burn incense to the Queen of Heaven, and shall pour her libations as we used to do . . . in the cities of Judah, in the streets of Jerusalem. For then we had plenty of food, and we were all well and saw no evil. But since we ceased burning incense to the Queen of Heaven and to pour her libations, we have wanted everything and have been consumed by sword and famine." (RSV 44: 16-18)

But *Cakes* is not a course about the Bible. It is about women reclaiming a much broader and very ancient lost heritage. It is also about relating that heritage to personal issues in women's lives. How we feel about our female bodies and our sexuality, how we feel about power, about mother-daughter relationships, about our competence and ability to act in the world.

As a woman, my religious history is rooted in the ancient pre-patriarchal world when the divine was imaged as a Great Goddess who gave birth to all of creation. Greeks and Romans, Minoans and Canaanites, Egyptians and Old Europeans—all worshipped Goddesses. I needed to claim that heritage. I needed to know that great civilizations were created by people who worshipped the divine as female. If the myths of a culture reflect its social arrangements, women must have had power and respect. The myths tell us that in very early times the Goddess reigned. I believe that men as well as women need to know that for many thousands of years of our human heritage God was female. In Judaism and Christianity as we have known them, there is only the father or the father and son. According to archeologist Raphael Patai, even Yahweh had a female partner for many centuries, but she has been very effectively edited out of the scriptures. Christianity exalted Mary for awhile, but never in Protestantism.

Cakes for the Queen of Heaven was published by the Unitarian Universalist Association in 1986, and it has had an amazing impact on many women. I think it started us on a spiritual journey. New things happened when women came together to study our own history and to share our personal experiences with each other.

One thing that happened was that we discovered in ourselves a deep hunger for meaningful ritual. There is almost no ritual written into the original course. But as an educator I thought it would be useful to open and close each session by lighting a candle and reading a poem or singing a song related to the subject matter. For the first session I passed a candle around and asked each woman to say her own name, her mother's name, her grandmother's name and so on as far back as she knew the names. I thought it would get us acquainted and perhaps make us realize how few of the names we actually knew. What happened was far more emotional. Sometimes we had the feeling that saying the names aloud actually brought our female ancestors into the circle with us. We wanted to take some time to tell their stories.

We found that we needed ways to celebrate our bodies, our mothers and grandmothers, our daughters' first periods, and our own dreams for ourselves. I have been astonished over and over again by the beautiful altars and creative rituals designed by women. Why, I wondered do we need to do this? I think it's because the male-oriented myths and symbols used for worship in our congregations so often failed to touch us, change us, make us whole as women.

We also discovered that the old goddess religions honored the earth, its elements, its cycles, its animals and plants. I am probably the most urban person you can imagine, but there I was leaping over a bonfire on a hill overlooking San Francisco Bay, and dancing a spiral dance in a meadow in Wisconsin. We realized how desperately this honoring of the earth is needed today. The earth is in a severe crisis. Our water is polluted, our cities are choking on poisonous smog, the ozone layer has huge holes in it and our forests are disappearing. Something is terribly wrong with our attitudes toward these life-giving ecosystems, just as something has been terribly wrong with our attitudes toward ourselves as women.

We are talking about some basic thealogical questions here. Who am I as a female human being? What is my relationship with the universe? What will happen to me when I die? As women came together to study these questions in light of our ancient female religious history we felt compelled to ask what was the source of our destructive attitudes toward women and the earth.

Patriarchal societies all over the world have for centuries promulgated a world-view that can be imagined in the form of a ladder. God is at the top, below God are the angels, below them is man, below him is woman, below her are children and below them is the earth and its creatures. In this scheme higher is better, more important and in control of what is below. The material world, the earth and even our own bodies have been seen as inferior to an imaginary supernatural realm where some non-material part of us may go after death if we will just obey the authority above us. The divine in this view resides in the supernatural realm, not in the material world.

The biblical tradition gave man dominion over the earth as well as over women and children. Humanists lopped off God and the angels, but left the rest of the image in place. We have all learned to look upon the earth as a bundle of resources at the bottom of the ladder, resources to be exploited. Such a world-view undergirds the development of industries that pollute and human relationships that degrade and exploit. It condones and encourages the use of force. It generates resentment, hatred and war. How? Those at the top of the ladder are raised to believe that they have to fight to control everyone and everything below them on the ladder. Those below feel resentment or participate in their own degradation by believing themselves to be inferior.

Perhaps the most significant theological change in our liberal religion in the latter part of the twentieth century was the addition of a new principle to our agreed upon Unitarian Universalist Principles and Purposes. It is the one that says that we affirm "the interdependent web of all existence of which we are a part." It is interesting that Sophia Fahs pointed out that "balanced interdependence" long before we thought to include it in our principles. We have, it seems, replaced the hierarchical ladder with an interdependent web as our way of seeing ourselves and our world. We have also added earth-based traditions to our list of sources of inspiration. I notice however that there is still no mention of the insights of feminist thea/ology in our list of sources.

Many of the women who arrived in theological schools in the late seventies were already middle-aged. We had raised families or had other careers. Now we stand before you as Crones, women of wisdom and power. With our lay women sisters we have fomented a revolution in thea/ology.

In her book *Celebrating Her*, Wendy Hunter Roberts remarks, "Of all the signs on the horizon, perhaps the most interesting are the countless homegrown women's spirituality groups that have sprung up all across the nation and beyond." This phenomenon of "homegrown women's spirituality groups" has been especially widespread among feminists and within Unitarian Universalism. As women came together to study our own religious heritage using the *Cakes for the Queen of Heaven* course, many felt that the process changed our lives. Indeed as the author of *Cakes*, I received hundreds of notes from women all over the country, each one saying about the course, "It changed my life." As I entered my later years those affirmations in turn changed my life. What a gift to be told again and again that a work of mine had touched and changed so many lives! The UU Women's Federation even honored me with their Ministry to Women Award.

Let us not forget that it was the women in our congregations who stood up every time sexist language was spoken until the ministers and worship leaders changed the words. It was the women in our movement who demanded that sexist language not be part of our Principles and Purposes. It was the women who demanded a hymnal free of sexist language. It was the women who brought home from women's conferences and incorporated into Sunday worship the sharing of joys and concerns; the sharing of the waters collected on summer vacations; the arrangement of chairs in half circles rather than rigid rows; the closing words "Blessed be."

Most importantly, it was because of the women that a spirituality of personal experience and warmth of community across all thea/ological positions gradually began to replace the cool intellectual sermon. Women in "homegrown spirituality groups" made it happen. I hope we will continue to do so.

Chapter 12

The Goddess and Universalism

One year at General Assembly I was on a panel concerning the Goddess and Universalism. It was an opportunity to integrate feminist spirituality with the Universalist spiral of our heritage.

The original message of Universalism, that if God is Love then all are saved, signaled a major shift in the mythology of Western culture. It was a radical idea because it implied that all people have the potential for good—even women. No one is cast as the "other." It meant that as part of nature neither we nor the rest of the material world are by nature fallen and sinful. Instead, the divine potential for good lies within the whole of creation. Universalism opened the way to reclaiming respect for women and respect for the earth.

If women are saved, made with the potential for good because they are made in the image of the divine, then the divine must be imaged as female as well as male. This shift in mythology enabled us to look with new respect at the great goddesses of the ancient world. Women especially have been exhilarated to discover that the divine was thought of as female for many thousands of years. Women brought forth new life from their magical bodies which also provided nourishment for the newborn. It was logical to see the creator as a female who gave birth to the world and continued to feed it. She was also seen as the Crone whose cycles destroy life so that new life may emerge. Male gods came along later, often as sky gods and consorts of the Great Goddess. In our culture the sky god ultimately became the only god.

In the modern world it has been increasingly difficult to defend a god who is "in heaven," out there in space, not part of "his" creation. Such a myth no longer resonates with our world-view or our sciences. We can however identify with the divine as a journey into self-understanding. The divine is no longer a mythical being somewhere beyond our material world, but is perhaps the life, the potential for goodness and for death embodied in each of us, female as well as male.

Such a view of the divine, as embedded and embodied *in* the life and death cycles of the world, pushes us to look at all people, at other cultures, at indigenous traditions, with new respect. Such a view of the divine implies that all of creation is sacred, that the earth itself is to be treasured rather than exploited.

Universalism helped us to widen our identities, so that what had been most despised, namely women and the earth, could once again be included within the circle of the sacred. The symbol for this new valuing of women and the earth is the divine female, the Great Goddess, Gaia Herself.

Chapter 13

Meditation and Me

As I continued on my ministerial journey in later years as an Accredited Interim Minister, I discovered that more and more of our congregations had meditation groups, sometimes more than one. Or an occasional Sunday service, a large portion of which was spent in silent meditation or guided visualization. I sometimes tried to join in but never found it to be meaningful to me. Other people seemed to find both comfort and renewed energy as a result of meditation, but it did nothing but irritate me. Words, music, dance, even a few moments of silence to take in a new idea I found moving or helpful. But not being silent for a long time, and especially not being told what to imagine or what word to repeat to myself. As a minister I urged people to turn inward, to find within themselves the power and creativity to make life meaningful. I understood that many people took that journey inward by means of silent meditation. Why didn't it work that way for me? Whoever heard of a minister who didn't meditate?

Perhaps I never stayed with meditation long enough. Or maybe I was just odd. That old familiar notion of being odd should have been a clue, but I didn't get it until I read Carol Lee Flinders' book *At the Root of This Longing*. There she explores the conflict she felt between her meditative life and her feminism. She lists four instructions that all major meditation traditions give their practitioners:

1) Be silent. Curb speech, but still the mind as well, particularly thoughts of "I" and "my." "He who speaks does not know," says the Tao. "He who knows does not speak."
2) Put yourself last, or in the words of Thomas a Kempis, "Seek always the lowest place, and to be inferior to everyone." Unseat the ego.

3) Resist and rechannel your desires. Disidentify yourself with your body and senses. Learn, indeed, that your body does not belong to you.
4) Enclose yourself. Turn inward, and move into a protective "container." Disentangle yourself from as much external and public activity as you can.

Then she lists four instructions feminists give to women:

(1) Find your voice; tell your story, make yourself heard at the highest levels of every institution that affects your life.
(2) Know who you are. Establish your authentic identity or selfhood. Identify your needs and learn how to meet them.
(3) Reclaim your body, and its desires, from all who would objectify and demean it, whether it is the fashion industry, pornographers, or even the medical establishment. Recognize the hatred of the female body that pervades contemporary culture, and oppose it.
(4) Move about freely and fearlessly. Take back the streets. Take back the night and the day.

Flinders points out that women are already socialized to be quiet and to put the needs of others ahead of their own, to see their bodies as objects, to stay out of public life. She even recounts incidents of women not finding meditation helpful, and being angered by it. So once again in my life a burden of odd-ballness was lifted from me. Flinders finds ways to integrate her feminism and her meditative life. I am just glad to have learned the reason why meditation doesn't work for me. If asked about a "spiritual practice" I just tell people I keep a journal. And I do—every day at Peet's coffee shop. I never called my writing "meditation" but over the years I realized that in writing down my feelings and thoughts in my journal I often stumbled upon insights about myself, my relationships, my world. I have tried to express some of those insights in the sermons and writings I offer to others.

Natalie Goldberg who practiced Zen meditation for many years while becoming a successful writer, quotes her beloved Zen teacher as saying, "If you commit to it, writing will take you as deep as Zen." He also told her that someday she would have to choose, that "Writing and Zen are parallel paths, but not the same." Eventually she realized that she had chosen writing. Perhaps as feminists we choose to express the depth of female experience so often neglected in patriarchal traditions.

We find our true selves, however, not only through writing and other spiritual practices but even more powerfully through relationships. It is perhaps no accident that Goldberg devotes many pages of her memoir to describing the ways in which her teacher inspired and empowered her. Sometimes even brief moments of depth with others stay with us. In my twenties when I felt like such an oddball—a young mother in theological school—I experienced three such moments. At three separate social gatherings, three different middle-aged housewives (an aunt and two old friends of my parents) took me aside and whispered to me "You stay in school! When you get to be my age you'll be glad you did." That was all. Each walked away and returned to the party. But their words and the fierce look in their eyes have stayed with me to this day. It is not only our academic and professional teachers who reach our inner selves and empower us.

I enjoyed very much Suze Orman's presentation about Women and Money on public television. When she asks for questions from the audience, a woman goes to the microphone and softly mumbles her name. Suze then encourages her to say her name several times with more and more power and confidence. I found myself saying aloud to the TV, "Right on, Suze!"

from SHIRLEY'S CAULDRON

I was in London for a week with my daughter Laura and my old friend Maeona. One evening as we were walking back to our hotel from the nearby pub, we saw a strange looking animal walking down the sidewalk across the street from us. One of us said, "Too large for a cat." Another said, "Doesn't look like a dog." The third said, "What *is* that anyway?" As it came closer, we all said with one surprised voice, "That's a fox!" We didn't think we had that much to drink at the pub, but it was hard to believe our eyes. Back at the hotel we told the clerk about it and he just shrugged.

The next day the newspaper headline was about "slaughtered foxes." It seems that there are thousands of these critters living in London's parks and gardens and one man took a shot-gun and killed about eight of them.

On Sunday I visited the Essex Unitarian Church and at the coffee hour I mentioned the fox to a woman. She said, "Oh yes. There are so many! I have a very small garden but there is a fox that lives there. He comes out and suns himself from time to time."

Yes, we did the museums, St. Paul's Cathedral, the Globe Theater, Windsor Castle, and saw a play starring Diana Rigg. But I suspect that the most memorable event of our trip will be seeing a real live fox on a London sidewalk.

Blessed be!

SPIRAL FOUR

The Beauty of the Green Earth: the Environmental Imperative

I will sing of the well-founded Earth,
Mother of all, eldest of all beings
She feeds all creatures that are in the world,
all that go upon the goodly land,
all that are in the paths of the seas,
and all that fly;
all these are fed of her store.
Through you, O Queen, we are blessed
in our children, and in our harvest
and to you we owe our lives.
Happy are we, who you delight to honour!
We have all things abundantly:
our houses are filled with good things,
our cities are orderly,
our sons exult with everfresh delight
and our daughters with flower laden hands
play and skip merrily over the soft flowers of the field.
Thus it is for those whom you honour,
O holy Goddess, Bountiful spirit!
Hail Earth, mother of the gods,
freely bestow upon me for this my song
that cheers the heart!

-Homer

Hear the words of the Star Goddess, the dust of whose feet are the hosts of heaven, whose body encircles the universe:

"I who am the beauty of the green earth and the white moon among the stars and the mysteries of the waters, I call upon your soul to arise and come unto me. For I am the soul of nature that gives life to the universe. From Me all things proceed and unto Me they must return. Let My worship be in the heart that rejoices, for behold—all acts of love and pleasure are My rituals. Let there be beauty and strength, power and compassion, honor and humility, mirth and reverence within you. And you who seek to know Me, know that your seeking and yearning will avail you not unless you know this Mystery: If that which you seek, you find not within yourself, you will never find it without. For behold, I have been with you from the beginning, and I am that which is attained at the end of desire." (in Starhawk 1989)

Spiritual traditions which honor the earth—our second imperative as we continue into this new century. Our problem with the earth has much to do with our fear of death. In the old agrarian traditions death was a natural part of the life cycle. The dead became part of the rocks and the trees and the rivers. As male gods took over in mythology and men took over in society, they perceived the old Goddess of transformation and death to be the most dangerous aspect of the old religions. She was the crone, symbol of the fierce old woman. She had to be destroyed so that death could be conquered. Recycling was no longer good enough. We had to escape the cycle and live forever in some supernatural realm. Earthly life became but a preparation for eternal life. Gradually the earth, this life, our physical bodies, all became denigrated, compared unfavorably with the life of our so-called immortal souls.

The implications of this denigration of our earthly life are many. The earth was no longer sacred. We humans were seen as separate from the rest of life, more important because of our immortal souls. It became easy to see the earth as a bundle of resources put here for our use. The earth could be exploited, used, and the loss of resources not even included in the costs of doing our business. This attitude is carved so deeply into our imaginations that we have been unable even to admit that the holes in the ozone layer, or the loss of our forests, or the pollution of our water and air will affect us. These are after all only lowly material things. Only our disembodied souls are sacred.

There was a popular song years ago that summed up this theology. It said, "God is watching us, from a distance." To imagine the divine as something or someone watching us from a distance is to miss the very sacredness right here within our bodies and our cosmos.

Our challenge is to reclaim this earthly bodily life as sacred, as the only precious life we have. We need to reclaim the image of the Old Woman who brought transformation and death as a part of the cycle of life. We need to stop seeing ourselves as immortal souls separate from the rest of life. That means we need to stop pitting ourselves against nature because we can't win that way. To destroy the resources of the planet is ultimately to destroy our own life support system. The earth may find ways to survive and heal itself, but we humans may go the way of the dinosaurs.

What does it mean to perceive the earth as sacred? It means taking seriously our own principle that we affirm respect for the interdependent web of all existence of which we are a part. We have also added another line to our Principles and Purposes. It lists another source of our inspiration and wisdom as "Spiritual teachings of Earth-centered traditions which celebrate the sacred circle of life and instruct us to live in harmony with the rhythms of nature." We have this priceless freedom to draw on many traditions. Right now we need very much to remind ourselves and proclaim to the world that we look to earth-honoring traditions for their special wisdom.

Chapter 14

The Covenant of Unitarian Universalist Pagans

I personally came to the old pagan religions as a woman searching for my female roots. Other people are drawn to these old traditions because they are earth-based. In many parts of our country, pagan groups have formed and they are providing a religious alternative to Judaism, Christianity, Islam and the religions of Asia. Old myths are being re-told and reinterpreted to meet the needs and issues important to people today.

In 1987 at the General Assembly of the Unitarian Universalist Association in Little Rock, Arkansas, there were two workshops on pagan religion. At the end of the second one, a large number of people stayed to form a new organization: The Covenant of Unitarian Universalist Pagans. I served on the Board of that organization for several years. During that time we discovered that many Unitarian Universalists found witchcraft meaningful.

This revival and transformation of pagan traditions is of interest to feminists and to Unitarian Universalists in at least three ways:

The first is what we might call the internalization of religion. Contemporary pagans speak of the god or goddess within each of us. Their rituals are intended to awaken a heightened sense of wholeness and selfhood. Thou art Goddess, they say to each other. Thou art God. They practice a religion that places divinity within the person. Myths are accepted as ways of telling the story of our inner journeys. Each person is encouraged to explore her or his own experience and to find there the basis for values and commitments. Notice too that since the divine is experienced as internal, it is described in female as well as male terms.

In the Old Religions of the ancient world, for many thousands of years the chief deity was female because the female was experienced as the primary source of life. She was sacred. The rediscovery of this attitude toward the female as sacred has had an electrifying effect on many modern women. As pagan writer Starhawk points out, "The image of the goddess inspires women to see ourselves as divine, our bodies as sacred, the changing phases of our lives as holy."

Like the pagans UUs too tend to describe the divine as internal, as a spiritual journey toward full selfhood, toward awareness of our potential. We come together much as the pagan covens do, to share our stories, to work together on the questions we have about life.

The second way in which the contemporary pagan religion is of interest to us, is in its concern for the well-being of the earth. Just as the divine is within human beings as the shape of our creativity, so also is the divine immanent in all of nature. Pagans, like Unitarian Universalists, see themselves as interdependent or connected with every part of the natural world. Such a view has not been characteristic of Judaism or Christianity, the traditions which pervade most of our society. These traditions have tended to keep God separate from the world, and human beings separate from the rest of nature. We have taken the position either that God created us at the beginning of time to rule over nature, or that we have evolved as the ultimate achievement of nature and are therefore superior to all the rest and should be in control of it. Neither of these views does much to put us in harmony with the rest of nature. Both views in fact open the way for our exploitation of the earth.

Science today supports a view of the earth and perhaps the cosmos as a delicate balance of intricate connections. In this view we are all one, not only as humans, but as parts of a pulsating organism which is the earth. To exploit or damage the earth is to damage ourselves.

Pagans celebrate the cycles of nature, the seasons, the waxing and waning of the moon, the life stages of human beings. They combine these celebrations with a modern scientific understanding of the ways things change. Modern witchcraft wishes to be grounded in science, in careful observation of the physical world. Observation is meditation, as the builders of Stonehenge—temple, astronomical observatory, calendar and calculator—knew very well.

Starhawk suggests that a photograph of the earth as seen from space might be our mandala. We might meditate on the structure of the atom. We might see the years Jane Goodall spent observing chimpanzees as a spiritual discipline. Such an attitude is dear to the hearts of Unitarian Universalists who have long championed the cause of scientific inquiry.

For many people Christmas has become a celebration of the winter solstice and Easter the celebration of spring. In moving away from the idea of a divine savior, we have returned to the more ancient awareness of religion as our relationship not only with each other but with the cycles of the natural world. This emphasis is crucial if we are to avoid complete ecological disaster.

A third characteristic of pagan religion is its non-authoritarian attitude. Leadership is shared and there is no hierarchy. Freedom and responsibility for one's own life and beliefs is central just as it is for us. Do as you will, so long as you harm no one is the rule of pagan religion. There are no creeds, no scriptures handed down. The creativity within each person is tapped and new poetry, new meditations, new stories are written. This means of course that the leadership and creativity of women is valued equally with that of men.

Perhaps it should not surprise us that our Unitarian Universalist values make us kindred spirits with witches. Those values may seem familiar and comfortable to us but they are by no means accepted in the world at large. People, far from experiencing themselves as sacred, often feel that they are insignificant victims of political and economic forces. Terrorists continue to escalate their bombings; industries continue to pollute the air, the oceans and the land. Science, the careful observation of the natural world, still battles superstition in our public schools. And in this land of freedom and representative democracy, the equal rights amendment for women was never ratified.

We need tremendous inner strength and power, and many kindred spirits, to face the world with the values we profess: an understanding of the divine as residing in us and in all of nature as the creative potential; a profound concern for the earth; and a commitment to the potential of all persons to take responsibility for their own beliefs.

Chapter 15

Persephone Returns

One of the most exhilarating experiences I can think of is diving under a huge ocean wave which is about to come crashing down on your head. You dive deep into the quieter water. You barely feel the wave go over. You surface, and there you are facing another one. Down you go again, outwitting the powerful monster by going under it, by making use of the quiet depths. This image of diving is often used as a metaphor for exploring the depths of the personal unconscious, the deep longings and the emotional shipwrecks that lie beneath the conscious selves we present to the world. And that journey inward with all its fears and with all its rewarding insights about who I am and what meaning my life may have is seen by many of us today as analogous to the great mythic journeys of the deities and heroes of the past.

But the great mythic journeys were more than personal adventures and they carried more than personal meanings. They involved the acquisition of some treasure or understanding that would be brought home to the community for its well-being. So too with our spiritual journey. Diving is only part of the adventure. We also have to surface, to face the next wave, and eventually to ride one of those waves to shore bringing with us the hard won treasures to share with our community.

As a psychologist I was especially interested in the personal spiritual journey which can yield insights that make life meaningful. Like many women I was drawn to the myth of Demeter and Her Daughter Persephone. The Homeric *Hymn to Demeter*, assigned to the seventh century BCE, is a story written to explain the Eleusinian Mysteries, which honored Demeter. The tale became famous as "The Rape of Persephone," who was carried off to the underworld and forced to become the bride of Hades. However, according to classical scholar Charlene Spretnak, there was no mention of rape in the ancient religion of Demeter and Her Daughter prior to the Olympian version of the myth. Evidence indicates that this twist to the story was not part of the original mythology. In Spretnak's re-telling of the pre-Hellenic version of the myth, Persephone makes her own decision to explore the depths of the underworld and visit the spirits of the dead. She returns each spring to her mother as all of nature celebrates.

It is difficult to describe the intense shock of recognition and anger that I felt as a woman at the moment when I realized that in contrast to Christians, who worship a divine *father* and *son*, the pilgrims who made their way to Eleusis for 2000 or more years worshipped a divine *mother* and *daughter*. The medium is indeed the message. All the teachings of love and justice in the world could not erase or make up for the stark and overwhelming absence of the divine female in my Protestant Christian upbringing.

Try to grasp the immensity of the fact that the chief divine actors in this drama were a mother and her daughter. Persephone decides she must leave her mother and embark on her own spiritual journey. This journey has its antecedents in the spiritual quest of the Sumerian Goddess Innana, who also descended to the underworld. Demeter fears for her daughter, grieves at her absence, is angry and forbids new life to grow, but knows that the journey is necessary. Ultimately Persephone returns to her mother, transformed into an adult by her journey, and they rejoice in a new kind of relationship.

In the later patriarchal version of the myth, Persephone is captured and carried off by force; she does not make her own decision, and Demeter is more angry than aggrieved. The daughter is never allowed to grow into her true self, and her relationship with her mother is strained and arbitrary.

As women raised in a patriarchal society we often have terrible problems in our mother-daughter relationships. As tiny children both girls and boys in Western cultures must separate from their mothers and go into what has traditionally been perceived as the world of their fathers—even though most mothers have always worked outside the home. Mothers are still our primary caretakers and in order to separate we reject them. In addition, psychology and sociology often have blamed mothers for every problem imaginable. Both young men and young women are taught to blame and reject their mothers far more than they do their fathers. But women often have an added reason for resenting their mothers: by accepting society's stereotypes of women, some mothers have inadvertently collaborated in the stunting of their daughters' growth. As women we are all daughters, and only by becoming fully adult can we return to our mothers and establish an adult-to-adult relationship.

When adults enter psychotherapy it is often the case that their problems stem from unresolved conflicts with their parents. The first big step in therapy is often the total rejection of a parent, really telling your mother or father off. Not only is it painful for everyone, it is only the first step. At some point a new relationship must come into being, one in which parent and child face each other as adults. Very often we think our problem is with the father because we have rejected mother much earlier in life. But when we dig deeper we may discover that it is our old longing for that rejected mother that needs to be resolved. What has to happen then is that we face that mother, in real life if she's still alive or within ourselves if she's not, and reclaim her love, not as the mother of an infant but as a wise woman we might like to have for a friend. Just as Persephone returned each year to be with her mother Demeter, we need to reclaim the Goddess as a symbol of our earliest religious history, but more importantly as a loving power within ourselves.

Another reason some women may fail to grow up is that only young women are considered desirable or valued in our society. Older women often try to look young because they know they are not wanted if they are old. This attitude was not part of the ancient Goddess religions. These myths and metaphors celebrated not only the Maiden and the Mother but also the Crone or wise old woman who had much to teach.

Let us then begin the journey into our authentic selves, into the energies which will free us from the stereotypes and the hatreds which bind us. From the dark, cold, difficult places on our journey, let us return like Persephone with new insights, new hopes, new life.

Chapter 16

Kermit, Transylvania and the Rainbow Connection

One of the most interesting experiences on my journey was a visit to Transylvania. I was serving as Interim Minister for two years at the Unitarian Universalist Church in Olympia, Washington. The congregation had a partner church in Kissoylmos. The Partner Church Council was planning a trip to Transylvania so that church members and clergy from a few congregations could meet their partners there. I decided to go and one of our members did too. It was a two-week tour. One week was spent visiting beautiful or famous places like the Dracula Castle as well as visiting the Unitarian theological school in Kolossvar. And there was the sarcophagus of King John Sigismund whose mother Queen Isabella issued the first known Edict of Religious Toleration in 1557. When her young son became king (the only Unitarian king in history) he reconfirmed the edict. Unitarians everywhere are proud of that edict, issued at a time when most Christian denominations were busy burning each other at the stake over their differences. I had read about the edict but being there gave it new meaning. I couldn't help but wonder what gave that Queen and her son the insight and the courage to take such a stand at that point in history. Even today some 450 years later we still struggle to live up to that ideal.

The other week was spent visiting our partner churches. In Kissoylmos I felt as if we had traveled back in time. Oh yes, there were phones and TVs and the minister had a computer, but the only car in the village belonged to the minister. The congregation was busy building a garage for it. I noticed that these farmers all lived in town and their farmlands stretched out around the town. My only experience of farms was as a child visiting in the Midwest of the United States where farm houses were separated sometimes by miles and the towns were mainly for shops. Of course the farms in Kissoylmos were much smaller, but I wondered if their system gave them more of a sense of community.

Another surprise for me, the quintessential urbanite, was the way each home had built onto it a small three-sided barn. I stood there smiling and saying to myself, "It's just like a Christmas crèche!" There was a cow, some chickens, a manger; all that was needed was the holy family. Every morning the cows strolled down the main street to their pasture and every evening they strolled back when the church bell rang, each cow seeming to know her own house. I felt as if we had stepped into a centuries-old way of life, that kings and conquerors and governments had come and gone but this agricultural life had survived it all and would continue to do so. We might help them with our money but they gave us a great gift of hope.

We visited the elementary school where the children were learning English. They already knew both Hungarian and Romanian. They sang for us the one song they knew in English—Happy Birthday. We showed them pictures of Olympia and the salmon which is so important in that area. On another day the village women came to the minister's home to show us how to do the beautiful embroidery they do. I think they were surprised to see how difficult it was for us. The men, not to be outdone, took us by horse-drawn cart to their still at the edge of town. There we sampled the brandy-like drink, Palinka, which they make there. I could almost hear my father saying from his grave, "Can we import some of that?" When we returned home we found that indeed someone does import a very similar drink. We served it when we reported back to the congregation about our trip.

As a minister visiting a partner church one is expected to present the sermon at the Sunday church service. The only requirement was that it must be based upon a Bible story or verse. I was very interested in pagan spirituality and because of its close relationship to nature it always seemed to me to be related to the amazing discoveries of postmodern science. I decided to talk about rainbows so I used the Genesis story of the rainbow which appeared in the sky after Noah and his ark survived the floods. I also took my Kermit-the-Frog puppet along and told how he sang a song about rainbows. The young minister, who translated my words into Hungarian as I spoke, liked Kermit so much that I left him there perched on the minister's computer in Kissoylmos.

When Kermit sang his song about rainbows I couldn't help but wonder if there really was something we had lost and might find once again. "Someday we'll find it," he sings "the rainbow connection, the lovers, the dreamers and me." Was Kermit right? Is there a rainbow connection? With all due respect to Kermit, the idea is certainly not new. In the biblical book of Genesis there is the story of Noah and his wonderful ark. When the rain stopped and the floods receded, a rainbow appeared and Noah heard God say "This is the sign of the covenant which I make between me and you and every living creature that is with you, for all future generations: I set my bow in the cloud and it shall be a sign of the covenant between me and the earth." In Japanese mythology the rainbow was believed to be the bridge by which the gods and goddesses came to the earth.

But Kermit's song is correct in suggesting that most of us today have lost the rainbow connection. The old myths no longer speak to us as powerfully as they once did. Can there be a new connection for us? We seem to keep searching. Is there some special knowledge or wisdom that we seek? If so, how do we go about finding it?

I like the rainbow because it puts us immediately in touch with two very different avenues to the special knowledge we seek, the avenue of science and the avenue of ideals and values. I like the term "connection" because it suggests that the wisdom we seek lies in relationships—among people, between people and the earth, and among all the roads we travel as individual searchers.

The rainbow itself is a natural phenomenon. It doesn't require the intervention of supernatural powers or extraordinary circumstances. I look out my window. The rain has let up, the sun comes out and shines through the raindrops which act like prisms breaking the light up into the spectrum of colors and there it is—a magnificent arc of colors across the sky. Of course an important part of that description is the eye looking out the window. It can be argued that the rainbow is an illusion because a creature with a different type of eye would see something different. A color blind person perhaps experiences rainbows quite differently from the way I do. So it isn't just the sunlight broken up by the raindrops. It's my eye that receives the colorful image and my brain that organizes that information into an impressive arc and labels it a rainbow.

So the description of a rainbow really isn't complete without a description of my eye and my brain. Does that mean I'm part of the rainbow? Imagine that! Of course one could also say that a description of me is incomplete without the details of what my eyes and my brain do with sunlight shining through raindrops in the sky. Does that mean that the rainbow is part of me? Well, I don't know. But the complex scientific data all by themselves seem to suggest at the very least that I am physically connected with rainbows. And that amazes and awes me.

I suggest that one road to the special wisdom we seek is an understanding of contemporary science. We have a strong heritage of respect for science as a means of understanding ourselves and our world. But in recent years arrogant human beings armed with limited scientific knowledge have gone about tampering with ecosystems with alarming results. The problem is that we have retained an outmoded world-view which held that we are separate from and superior to the rest of nature, or at the very least, the pinnacle of evolution. It is not scientific knowledge that is at fault but rather our unwillingness to accept the world-view that more recent knowledge brings.

Post-modern science revealed a world in which cooperation among organisms is the rule and an awesome potential for novelty is built into the system. Some of the best sermons are being written today by scientists, people involved every day in the minute details of microbiology, subatomic physics or the far reaches of space-time. They are rediscovering mystery, wonder and humility before the intricate complexity and necessary connectedness of every event in the universe.

The rainbow connection means that you and I are part of that connectedness.

Rainbows are also intimately involved in social science which attempts to understand human behavior and motivation. Because rainbows occur just as the skies clear after a storm, just as the sun begins to shine through the clouds, we humans have made of the rainbow a symbol of hope. We wonder what new possibilities lie on the other side of the rainbow, in our future. We look at the beautiful arc of colors and all our cherished ideals come to mind. Even if you know that ideals by definition can never be fully realized, you may get a lift and a surge of energy at the thought that if there are rainbows then perhaps some positive change is possible. I think the rainbow as a symbol causes us to look inward and to ask some ultimate questions about what it is we value and where we choose to direct our life energies.

One of the hardest lessons scientists of all kinds have had to learn is that the experimenter, the person doing the research, affects the results. This is true even in the hard-nosed physical sciences but it is especially important in the social sciences. There are limits to objectivity. Who I am affects the kinds of questions I ask and the methods or measurements I use as well as my interpretation of the results. To put it another way, in order to understand any natural event, particularly one involving people, we have to turn the spotlight on ourselves as part of the process. That can be very uncomfortable because the sad truth is that so many of us, even when we do look inward, forget to ask ourselves the hard questions, like "How does the world really look to me?" Or how do *I* feel about going to college or getting married or whatever the rest of the world is currently expecting me to do or be? It's so much easier just to go along doing what's practical and expected, following the leader, or as one of our rainbow songs puts it, "follow the fellow who follows the dream." I say forget it! You follow your own dream!

It's been very hard for me to do that. I'm practical and agreeable and inclined to go along with what people expect of me if it seems reasonable—even when I don't like what I'm being asked to do. Me, take seriously my own thoughts and feelings and dare to articulate them? Who am I to be doing that? Haven't I just gone on at length about our connectedness and a scientific world view of cooperation among organisms? Shouldn't I be agreeable and practical and cooperative? Maybe not.

I have to tell a story about my father. He was a rather gruff businessman and he couldn't stand to hear that someone was nice. He would scowl and say "Nice! That's the worst thing you can say about anyone!" That used to irritate me because I was expending so much energy trying to be nice. But I think he may have been in touch with one of the most important discoveries of psychology—that niceness can be a wall we put up to hide our real feelings. The tragedy is that one can fool oneself into believing that the wall of niceness is her real self. It's a terrible thing to become a wall.

It can be frightening to look inward and to encounter our own real feelings. The frightening part is that being true to yourself often puts you in sharp disagreement with others. Especially if you are a member of an oppressed group there may be heavy risks involved when you start being authentic, even a little bit authentic. The rainbow connection means that we as individuals have to take the risk, look inward and clarify and express our dreams and values. The rainbow connection is a religious quest, an attempt to explore our relationships with the rest of nature, with each other and with our own inner selves.

Chapter 17

Spirals

In the fall of the year my reflections upon Halloween and our understanding of time bring me back again to the spiral symbol.

On Halloween we playfully re-enact a very ancient celebration. We climb the steps and enter the haunted house where death is portrayed in all its macabre and frightening glory. We gaze upon make-believe corpses and touch various wet and sticky substances as we are told they are the innards of the dead. We show that we are not afraid, that we can look at the symbols of death and laugh. Children dress up as ghosts and witches and haunt the streets after dark. Then we join our friends and bob for apples. Apart from the fun of it all, where did we get these strange customs and what do they mean?

Halloween has to do with our understanding of time. In the ancient world-view time was perceived as a cycle, always changing but also always repeating as do the cycles of nature, such as the seasonal changes, and the waxing and waning of the moon. Death was perceived as part of this endless cycle. Since the cycle did repeat, those who had died were considered still to be a part of the community although they now lived in another form. Often the dead were buried right beneath the homes of the living and their names and deeds were spoken of and woven into the ongoing life of the community.

On one night each year, at the time of the death of the waning year, the gates between the living and the dead were felt to open more fully. On that night the dead were said to return to be honored or reborn. On that night the living acted out in ritual the journey over the sunless sea which was death, and the breaking of the bonds which was transformation and rebirth. The pomegranate symbolized the ritual death, the apple the ritual rebirth. The living were thus reminded that they too would change and die and return to be honored and reborn. The natural cycle of death followed by new life in the seeds of trees and grain was thought to be the natural pattern for human beings as well.

The Christian Church was unable to stamp out the old pagan religions by burning people at the stake, so it adapted pagan holidays to its own uses. On Halloween it kept the idea that the dead were still part of the community and set aside November 1, as All Saints Day, a time to honor all the Christians who had lived and died. In Hispanic countries November 2 is often designated the Day of the Dead. Because Christianity postulates a separate supernatural realm where the souls of the dead are said to exist, Halloween, or the night before All Saints Day became a time of supernatural intervention, when the dead from that other world returned to haunt this world as ghosts. The connection with the cycles of nature was lost and as modern science dispelled belief in the supernatural, Halloween became a time of play, a time to laugh at death. The pomegranate has disappeared from the festivities, but the apple remains.

But what of our understanding of time? We no longer view time in terms of cycles that repeat. We teach children history by constructing time lines. Events are seen as following each other in an endless straight line from the beginning of time on into the infinite future. We have discovered that life does not go on endlessly repeating but that instead it has evolved and changed and brought forth more and more complex forms.

In the 20th century however, we had to face a new problem about time—the idea of its relativity. Time out in space is not the same as time measured on the earth. Indeed, if you go out into space for a period of time and then return, more earth-time will have passed while you were gone than has passed for you on your journey. When you return you will be younger than you would have been had you stayed on the earth. Someone has figured out that if you could stay out in space for fifty years as measured by you on your journey, you would return to earth and find that some three hundred years had passed. Science fiction has had a marvelous time with that idea. It does shake up our notions of time as either a circle or a straight line. Neither the circle nor the straight line will do as a representation of time for us.

Paganism today provides us with an alternative way to view time, as a spiral honoring the cycles of nature yet encompassing as well the ever-changing evolving nature of the cosmos. The spiral as well as the circle was in fact used as a symbol of death and rebirth in ancient times, but our understanding of that symbol, the spiral, is deepened today as we recognize the spiral as the shape of the DNA molecule which sets the pattern for an organism's growth, and as the shape of the galaxy itself.

The spiral appeared again when I went to the Unitarian Universalist congregation in Williamsburg, Virginia to serve as Interim Minister. Imagine my surprise when I entered the sanctuary there and saw a large copper spiral prominently displayed in an acrylic case up in front. Inspired by the spiral shape found in the ocean's chambered nautilus and in the strands of our DNA, the artist, Pat Winter, chose the spiral as a visible symbol of the life and growth of the congregation. Each year on Charter Sunday a new marker is bolted into the spiral to celebrate that year's life and growth. At the same time one can see the still-empty holes waiting to mark the life and growth of the future.

from SHIRLEY'S CAULDRON

A few years ago a good friend gave me a small pin—a road runner. She said it seemed to be my symbol, always on the road as I moved from one interim ministry to another. I do love to drive. I-80 and I are old friends—and large segments of I-90, I-70, I-40, I-10, I-5—you get the picture.

My wanderings have given me the opportunity not only to enjoy the varied scenery of this country, but also to live with and know an incredible variety of Unitarian Universalist congregations and individuals. Everywhere I have found an instant community of kindred spirits joyfully struggling to uphold UU values and to reach out to the communities around them.

I have also attended a great variety of Canvass Dinners. In Mobile, Alabama there was a catered dinner of steaming seafood gumbo. The next year I knew I was in California when the Marin Fellowship in San Rafael brought in silver tureens of tofu and vegetables for their canvass dinner. In Reno, Nevada we rented a big room at one of the casinos where the parking was free and the fancy food remarkably inexpensive. The casino probably lost money on us as nobody bothered to do any gambling.

In Olympia, Washington even very urban people like to think they really belong in the country. The canvass dinner was in an old grange hall where the pagan group magically pulled dollars out of a steaming cauldron and there was a live caller for square dancing for all ages after dinner. In Oak Park, Illinois we had a pre-dinner cocktail party with chamber music in architect Frank Lloyd Wright's dramatic studio. In West Redding, Connecticut we donned evening clothes and took over a very elegant museum restaurant for the evening. And in Houston, Texas we enjoyed some excellent Mexican food at Tequila Willie's.

Blessed be!

SPIRAL FIVE

A Symbol for Our Times: the Multi-Cultural Imperative

The multi-cultural imperative calls us to set aside other unexamined assumptions—that light is better than dark, that bull-dozing the sacred lands of indigenous people does not interfere with their freedom to practice their religion, that it is superstition to believe that the ancestors have become part of the earth, the water and the trees. What are we assuming here? That our culture, our religion, our values are the highest, the best that human beings have created. Our language in its use of light and dark is just one indication of the assumptions carved into our imaginations.

It has been fascinating to me to learn that many of the indigenous spiritual traditions around the world, although patriarchal in many ways, have retained strong elements of honoring woman and honoring the earth. In the past we have called those traditions primitive but now we find that they have important truths to teach us. One truth found in many traditions is respect for the old women, the grandmothers of the community. They are often considered to have special wisdom and are granted the power to make important decisions and judgments for the whole community. Old women make up the fastest growing segment of our own population. How many do we see in positions of power? What would they bring to such positions if their wisdom was respected?

We can no longer afford to romanticize or demonize other cultures. Our task is to get to know each other as human beings searching in our own peculiar ways for the same creature comforts, fulfillment and satisfaction. We need to affirm more effectively our

UU principle of world community with peace, liberty, and justice for all.

Are there diverse cultures in your community? How well do you know them? What might the old women have to teach us?

Chapter 18

Walking Together

Centuries ago the Hebrew prophet Amos posed a question that still haunts us today. He asked, "Can two walk together except they be agreed?"

Answering yes to that question is not only the idealistic quirk of our small religious movement—Unitarian Universalism. It is a cornerstone of the United States Constitution. A right guaranteed there by the First Amendment. And it was the fervent hope of the post-World War II generation that the establishment of the United Nations would enable nations to walk together in peace, even when they disagreed. As terrorism escalates around the world, our faith in that ideal is being sorely tested.

We Unitarian Universalists are the religious group which has most clearly embraced diversity as an ideal, as a part of our covenant with each other. And yet we have had disputes and crises throughout our history which indicate that in the midst of controversy we often lose sight of our ideals. As Unitarian theologian Conrad Wright points out ". . . some of the most dramatic moments in our history have occurred when our tolerance for diversity wore very thin, and we were challenged to live up to the principles we proclaimed."

When Ralph Waldo Emerson delivered an address at Harvard Divinity School in 1838, Professor Andrews Norton called it "the latest form of infidelity" and "an insult to religion." Why was he so incensed? The prevailing view among Unitarians at that time was that Christianity was a divinely revealed religion and that it was proved to be so by the New Testament miracles. Emerson and the young Theodore Parker declared that "religion is not a matter of proof from the evidence of historical events, but is grounded in an inner religious consciousness." They insisted that Christianity was true only to the extent that it was an authentic expression of a *universal religious impulse* that all religious people share. Universal, going beyond even the boundaries of Christianity.

One hundred years later Sophia Fahs made important contributions to our awareness of other traditions. Her multi-cultural perspective prepared the way for our Unitarian Universalist acceptance and celebration of diversity. Her book *Beginnings of Earth and Sky*, a collection of creation stories from around the world was published in 1938. It includes the biblical story as one among many. Her book *From Long Ago and Many Lands*, another collection of religious stories from around the world was first published in 1948. In the introduction she writes that an important principle in selecting the stories for this collection "has been to choose stories from a wide variety of different cultures, races and religions so that early in life children may begin to feel some of the human universals that bind us together in a common world kinship. Our finest moral and spiritual ideals have been shared by many peoples."

Fahs was also a realist. She continues, "The emphasizing of ideals, however, has not led us to discard stories merely because they picture life's tragedies and evils. None of the people described in these stories should be presented as perfect. Children should know at an early age that all humans are imperfect. Learning from the past should mean learning by one's mistakes as well as by one's achievements."

In the 20th century we were challenged when large numbers of humanists joined our churches, non-theists, people who did not believe in a supernatural God, but did believe in our human potential for goodness and ethical living. The civil rights movement called upon us to acknowledge the racism deeply ingrained in many of our old assumptions. The women's movement urged us to root out the sexism in our theologies, our language and our organizational structures. Gay and lesbian and transgendered people, rejected by so many other traditions, came into our churches hoping we really meant the acceptance we proclaimed.

We have continued to affirm that yes, we can walk together and respect not only a variety of views but a variety of persons. But it has never been easy and some years ago we were faced with a new challenge. A pagan group in the Chicago area became interested in Unitarian Universalism when one of its members decided to enter the

UU ministry. The group gradually became excited about the idea of being part of our movement. Finally they applied to be affiliated with the Unitarian Universalist Association as a regular congregation. They issued a statement describing how their own values were in keeping with the principles and purposes of the UUA. They assumed, rightly, that they and we could walk together. They were indeed accepted, but not without controversy. One distinguished UU minister wrote a letter to many leaders in the denomination strenuously objecting to having a group of witches accepted as a congregation. The Board of Trustees of the UUA which votes on such applications did approve this one—but not unanimously.

Today there are pagans and pagan groups within most of our congregations. We come through, we stand by our principle of diversity, but not easily, not without some misgivings.

The truth is, we seem to need our boundaries even if we are called upon to expand them from time to time. Conrad Wright points out that any community must have some common goals or purposes, a value system generally accepted, a consensus widely shared, in order to survive. We have our principles and purposes document so we do in fact have some implied boundaries. The really important point is that those boundaries change. The consensus that unites us today is not the consensus that united us in the 19th century, nor the one that united us in the middle of the 20th century.

We have expanded our boundaries in many directions. We have learned to walk with more and more diversity. Is this not the over-riding lesson we must learn from the slaughters, the holocausts of our times? We are haltingly and with difficulty learning to listen to each other. Bombs are still being made, troops are still massed along old borders, hatred and bigotry are still preached, violence still erupts in our schools and churches. Even our own armed forces cannot stop the waves of terrorism washing over our world. But the very earth cries out that if we do not change we may not survive. Can we change?

An interesting attempt to listen to each other across some religious boundaries was made by a professor at Hebrew Union College in Cincinnati. He invited leaders from a variety of religious traditions to meet with him and to form what he called the Polydox Confederation. His view was that we could continue to enjoy the richness of our diverse religions but also create ways to be together.

We could discuss our human situation and more importantly we could create celebrations for special moments in our lives. Celebrations not based upon any of our particular traditions. Celebrations which we could all embrace. I joined the group and it was interesting to me how often we turned to nature to help us affirm life and growth and relationship without reference to our own religious traditions.

I would suggest to you that we can believe in freedom and diversity only if we believe in the positive as well as the negative potential of human nature, and indeed all of life. And that is precisely our heritage as Unitarian Universalists, as feminists, as Americans. It is because of that faith in our positive potential that we have chosen to walk together in diversity, to keep redefining and expanding our boundaries. We have chosen again and again to be inclusive, to recognize and accept people of good will wherever they are found and whatever they may be called—even witches.

I have long loved these words by Theodore Parker: "Be ours a religion which like sunshine goes everywhere; its temple, all space; its shrine, the good heart; its creed, all truth; its ritual, works of love; its profession of faith, divine living."

Chapter 19

The Chalice

When I read Riane Eisler's book *The Chalice and the Blade*, I was struck by her use of the chalice in the title as a symbol of the partnership model of social organization, and the blade as a symbol of the dominator model. I have watched the growing use of the chalice symbol in Unitarian Universalism. In the process of widening and changing our spiritual identities, I have come to see the chalice as a beautiful and universal symbol of the new religion which is emerging, and a symbol of past spirals of human experience in which the best of our human potential appeared.

Some years ago I visited the Cherokee Museum in Tahlequah, Oklahoma. The museum tells the story of the bitter march that the Cherokee people were forced to make all the way from North Carolina to Oklahoma, a march on which one quarter of their people perished. In the center of the museum is a magnificent sculpture titled Exodus. It is made in the form of two large tear drops. Into one tear drop is carved the anguished and suffering face of a Cherokee woman. Into the other tear drop is carved the child she carries on her back. The title of course refers to the biblical Exodus when the Hebrew people left their bondage in Egypt and set out on their journey across the desert to the land of Canaan.

As I thought about the sculpture, I saw that it represented a recurring theme: the endurance of unspeakable oppression and the repeated attempts by human beings to free themselves from this agony. Like the Cherokee sculptor, African Americans often identify strongly with the biblical exodus as they too celebrate their rise from slavery. Women articulate the oppression we experience and revel cautiously in hard won freedoms. Even the most privileged among us have felt some slings and arrows and can identify with the oppressed.

Why, I wondered. Why are we always having to protest, to rebel, to escape?

I would suggest to you that we have forgotten our deepest, oldest roots. We have lost thousands of years of human history and prehistory. We need to remember. In the words of Monique Wittig, "There was a time when you were not a slave, remember that. You walked alone full of laughter, you bathed bare bellied. You say you have lost all recollection of it, remember . . . you say there are no words to describe it, you say it does not exist. But remember. Make an effort to remember. Or, failing that, invent."

It is only in recent years that we have begun to pay attention to our ethnic needs to know who we are, where we came from and what we once stood for. To know what was lost when the oppressor took over. At Tahlequah I was shocked to discover that the names of the Cherokee founders of that city were all English and their pictures showed them in the standard European clothing of their time. They had already put aside their own ways and adopted those of the oppressor. All but one. The man called Sequoia. He is shown in traditional Cherokee garb and he is one of the heroes of today's Native Americans who are eager to reclaim their own traditions. When Sequoia learned from white people that language could be written down, he constructed a set of symbols, one for each sound in his native language. He then taught his people to use the symbols and in a matter of months, most of the community was literate. Sequoia even started a newspaper all written in his own language.

African Americans are tracing and honoring their African heritage. Women are looking into the mists of prehistory to a time when even God was female and women played important roles in every area of society. All of us are finding a wealth of lost wisdom about how to get along with each other and with nature.

Myths and legends from many cultures around the world tell of an earlier time when men and women lived in peace. The Hebrew Bible describes a garden where peace reigned—until a male god decreed that one person, the woman, be subservient to the other, the man. The Chinese Tao Te Ching describes a time when the wisdom of the Great Mother was honored above all. The Greek poet Hesiod wrote of a golden race who tilled the soil in peaceful ease before a lesser race brought in their god of war. Scholars agree that these stories are probably based on real prehistoric events and yet these references to a time when human beings lived in peace have usually been shrugged off as mere fantasy.

Today, however, a revolution has taken place in archeology. Evidence is mounting that these stories such as our expulsion from the Garden of Eden are real folk memories of the first agrarian societies, the people who planted the very first gardens. The legend of Atlantis, the beautiful civilization which sank into the sea is now believed to be a memory of the last days of the Minoan civilization on the island of Crete when the Greek islands were hit by major earthquakes and tidal waves.

The excavation of these ancient sites, according to one scholar, "reveals a long period of peace and prosperity when our social, technological and cultural evolution moved upward: many thousands of years when all the basic technologies on which civilization is built were developed in societies that were not male dominant, violent or hierarchic." Almost universally they viewed the universe as an all-giving mother and qualities such as caring, compassion and non-violence appear to have been highly valued. The social structure was neither matriarchal nor patriarchal. Scholars are suggesting that it may have been more of a partnership. Imagine that! A partnership!

There came a time however when our cultural evolution was interrupted. Invaders from peripheral areas gradually brought in and enforced a very different form of social organization—that of domination. These were people who worshipped the lethal power of the blade, the power to take life, the ultimate power needed to establish and enforce domination. In the millennia since then, the kind of society that has become entrenched around the world is based upon the principle of domination.

The Old Order, the partnership of caring, compassion and non-violence was not crushed easily or quickly. Many of its symbols and values have survived, mostly as the undercurrent of protest and rebellion against oppression.

The cup or chalice has been perhaps the most universal and persistent symbol of the Old Order. The earliest ritual of human beings may have been the sharing of food and drink. The cup or chalice appears in the myth of Themis as the ancient goddess convenes the deities and presides over their feasts. Jesus fed the multitudes and shared bread and wine with his disciples before he was arrested. It is interesting that while the chalice has survived as an important element in Christianity, the central symbol of that religion became the cross of death. But scholars today suggest that the cross or crucifix did not become central until a thousand years after Jesus' death. In another culture, Guru Nanak, founder of the Sikh religion, challenged the rigid caste system of his culture by insisting that all his followers of whatever caste should eat from the same bowl.

Unitarian Universalists have our own rather interesting history with the chalice. In the early days of World War II, the Unitarian Service Committee was formed to help Unitarians escape from Europe. As the full horror of the Nazi regime began to be understood, and as more and more of Europe fell, the Committee expanded its activities and helped a great variety of persons, including hundreds of children to escape. The task was especially difficult because of the many languages involved and the reluctance of most people to trust anyone.

In their office in Lisbon, the Service Committee leaders decided that they needed a symbol, some kind of sign they could use to identify themselves when making contact with people who needed to escape. One man working at the office had been helped to escape and he was an artist. He suggested a chalice, a flaming chalice, and he designed the logo for the committee. It worked well and many people liked it. After the war, as the Service Committee continued to expand its social justice activities, the chalice continued to be its symbol. To raise money the Committee had flaming chalice jewelry made and many Unitarians began to wear it.

Some years ago a group of Unitarian Universalist ministers was visiting Unitarian churches in Eastern Europe and some of the ministers were wearing flaming chalice jewelry. One of their hosts, who was also a Unitarian minister, noticed the jewelry and said, "I see you are wearing the flaming chalice. Is that a symbol used by American Unitarians?" The Americans then told her the story of the Service Committee and the artist who had designed the symbol for them.

The European minister laughed and said, "Well of course that artist knew very well what symbol to use. Surely you know about John Hus and the flaming chalice."

Jon Hus was born in Bohemia and educated at the University of Prague. He was ordained as a priest in 1401 and became a very popular and influential preacher. He protested the worldliness of the clergy and, like John Wycliffe in England, he wanted the Bible translated into the language of the people. But Jon Hus did something else. He began to serve the Communion wine to the people. Ordinarily they would receive only the bread, and priests were the only ones permitted to drink the wine. But John Hus offered the Chalice to everyone.

With such views and activities, he was soon in trouble. In 1414 he was ordered to appear before the Council of Constance to answer charges of heresy. The Council found him guilty of heresy and he was burned at the stake. Because of his great popularity among the people, his death set off civil wars in Bohemia and his followers used the chalice as their symbol. They added the flame to commemorate his death at the stake. The flaming chalice became a popular symbol throughout Eastern Europe, and was used repeatedly as a symbol of resistance to oppression. So of course the artist must have known this when he designed the symbol for the Service Committee.

We all have personal symbols, objects or pictures or quotations that have special meanings in our lives. But what about a symbol that other people might recognize, a symbol that carries a message of specific values, something we wish to lift up in the world as our stand, our commitment? If you were that artist, what symbol would you choose?

The Unitarian Universalist Association adopted the chalice as its symbol and gradually our congregations began to use it in worship services. Today every Sunday service and many committee meetings begin with the lighting of a chalice.

I believe it is time now for life-affirming symbols such as the chalice to function once again as the major symbols of our culture, and not just as signs of an undercurrent of protest. Our very future is at stake.

Chapter 20

Widening Our Identities

When I was studying at City College in New York City, I heard a special lecture by sociologist Gunnar Myrdal. He spoke to us in the midst of the civil rights movement and encouraged us to "widen our identities." The phrase stayed with me. Then one day my little son asked me, "Mom, how come when we have a white sitter we call her Mrs. and when we have a black sitter we call her by her first name?" I began to realize the insidious nature of our unconscious racism.

About twenty years ago I was sitting in Wendy's, drinking coffee and kind of absent-mindedly watching the customers come and go. All at once it hit me. I was in Jackson, Mississippi and all around me white and black people were eating peacefully together. The rest rooms too were for everyone. I realized that only about thirty years earlier as I sat in my New Jersey home watching the news on TV, young people were being beaten and dragged off to jail for trying to integrate lunch counters; armed men had to be called in to escort black children into previously white schools; freedom riders rode buses into the south refusing to abide by segregated seating laws, and a young black minister by the name of Martin Luther King, Jr. issued a call to clergy all over the country, asking them to come to the south and march with him demanding integration and civil rights for black people. Among those who responded to his call were three Unitarian Universalist ministers who were attacked one night and because no medical help was readily available, one of them died.

In 1965 the Unitarian Universalist church was the only place in Jackson where whites and blacks could meet together. And even that wasn't safe. The minister of the church was shot one night, right outside his home. He almost died, and fearing for the safety of his family, he left the state. The doors and windows of the church were repeatedly broken. But the church remained, and continued to be a center of support for the civil rights movement. The very first integrated Head Start nursery school program in Mississippi was held in that church.

By the time I arrived in Jackson in 1988 to be their part-time minister, the congregation had built a new small building. It had no sign and if you looked at it straight on from the street you could not see a door or a window. The front door was hidden behind a façade that blended in with the rest of the building. As for windows there was only one. It was for the office and it had bars and an alarm system. The main room, the sanctuary, had only clerestory windows way up high. They had built a little fortress and it took me a year to convince them that they should put a sign on the building.

As a result of that struggle, some laws did change. People can all eat together at Wendy's, use the same rest rooms and drinking fountains, and the schools technically are integrated. Segregation became de facto rather than de jure—just like it had always been in the north. I remember wondering forty-five years ago why people in the north were so willing to put their bodies on the line for integration in the south when as far as I could see we had never done anything to protest the kinds of segregation we had in the north. Of course the issue is more clear-cut when there is a specific law to be challenged. What we had all along in the north was a gentlemen's agreement.

I don't suppose very many people today remember that movie. A very old one called *Gentlemen's Agreement*. It had to do with anti-semitism rather than racism but the principle is the same. The young man in the movie was trying to document the discrimination he saw that Jewish people experienced. He sent two applications to a leading university, identical except that one went under the name of Green and the other under the name of Greenberg. Green was accepted; Greenberg was not. It was the same with country clubs. He might have been accepted of course if he had sacrificed his integrity and changed his name. But the bigotry was there. African Americans don't have that option because none of us can change the color of our skin.

The schools I attended in New Jersey were all integrated. So were the schools my father attended in the early years of the twentieth century. But a gentlemen's agreement was always in place. Together in school but still segregated outside of school. My father told me that his teachers taught those integrated classes that it was a fact that African Americans were inferior to whites in intelligence. "I often wondered," he said "what that did to those black kids, how they must have felt." They had stopped teaching that kind of misinformation by the time I went through the schools but counselors still advised black students to take the less demanding programs in high school. And of course the history and the literature and the culture we learned was all white and mostly male.

It is the winners, or more accurately, the conquerors who have written history and myths to support their views. And it is whites, specifically white men who have been the conquerors and the writers of our history and mythology for the past three to four thousand years. I was in graduate school before I was ever given the opportunity (much less required) to study black history and culture or women's history and culture.

As Unitarian Universalists we acknowledge the pluralism of the modern world and we refuse to accept any beliefs or values simply because they were handed down to us. We take responsibility for choosing what meanings we will affirm in life and of continuing to grow and change. We affirm what seems relevant and positive to us. Shelley Jackson Denham put her affirmation into a song and said, "We believe in life and in the strength of love and in the joy of being together." But often we are left with many questions.

Perhaps the biggest question is *how* to affirm life and love when all around us we see the signs of hatred—racism, sexism, war. Shootings, bombings, terrorism.

What does it mean to say that we believe in life and love and growth in such a situation? It means quite literally that one half of our brain doesn't know what the other half is doing. And that is exactly the reason why guilt never has worked. We are all in this together. The splitting of the atom enabled us to create nuclear weapons. It is the splitting of our personalities that has driven us to the edge of destruction. Only when that split within each of us is healed, only then do we have even a chance of affirming our positive potential.

Until we look, really look, at what we do with both sides of our brain, until we look, really look at what is happening around us, in our families, in our communities and in the world, we don't even know whether we are supporting good or evil.

It's easier not to look either inside or outside. The truth of our real feelings, the truth of our unwitting complicity in social evils, these are truths we would rather discover in someone else. Not only do we cut ourselves off from these truths about ourselves, we get rid of them by hanging them on handy scapegoats, usually groups of people we don't know too well. People in ghettos, people in distant countries, *them*. *They* are the bad ones. *They* want to destroy us. *We* only have bombs for defense.

In my lifetime we have often come to church and affirmed life and love and then gone out and supported a government which considered armaments more necessary than food. Perhaps we have reached some kind of turning point. We have in recent years sometimes sent our troops out to help feed people. Of course we have also bombed Afghanistan and Iraq. The journey toward universal human rights is complex and difficult.

If it is really up to us what happens in this society and on this planet, what are we going to do about life and love? Are we going to continue to allow our energy, our labor, our money, and many times our blood to be spent on pollution and on destruction? Our myths as we know them tell us that that is exactly what we have done and will do. History as we know it tells us the same. Who are we to say that human beings can change, can develop their potential for good?

Well, I believe we are people who are reclaiming many aspects of our human history that have been diminished, trivialized, or lost. My black history books go to great lengths in documenting the high and sophisticated civilizations created by black people in ancient Africa. My women's history books similarly document the glories of Crete and other ancient civilizations where women were central.

There is substantial agreement now among scholars that in ancient times, three to four thousand years ago there was indeed a patriarchal conquest as successive waves of nomadic Indo-European peoples swept south over Europe and the Middle East and India. Many of the older agricultural peoples who were conquered appear to have been darker-skinned, matrilinear and, most importantly, non-violent. In Egypt and in Crete, paintings show both dark and light-skinned people engaging in sports and sitting in positions of leadership.

With conquest came new myths, new gods, and revisions of history that diminish both blacks and women. More importantly, there came also a new attitude, a new mind-set in human relations—the idea that the rulers are superior and that they must defend their superiority by the use of force, and that there is no other way to organize society. These are the assumptions we have been carefully taught to accept and often we are not even aware of them.

Ever since those ancient conquests though, some human beings have sought to reclaim the power of love and non-violence and to establish equality among people of all kinds. Dr. Martin Luther King, Jr. was one of those people. African American leaders had worked for years trying to overturn laws that kept blacks from voting, trying to attack segregation, bringing cases into the courts year after year. They had some notable success as in the 1954 Supreme Court decision that segregated schools could not be considered equal.

But it was Martin Luther King who, in the words of historian Lerone Bennett, moved the struggle "from the courtroom to the streets, from law libraries to the pews of the churches, from the mind to the soul." King was a third generation Baptist preacher who inherited a tradition of protest. His grandfather had led a boycott against an Atlanta newspaper which spoke disparagingly of black voters, and was one of a group who pressured into existence Atlanta's first Negro high school. Martin Luther King, Jr. graduated from that high school and from Morehouse College. He also earned a Ph.D. in systematic theology from Boston University. Then he moved to Montgomery, Alabama.

In 1955 when Rosa Parks refused to give up her seat on the bus, she was arrested and the black community staged a one-day boycott of the buses in protest. The one-day boycott grew into a movement with King orchestrating the project, organizing car pools, holding pep rallies where hymns and spirituals were sung, and skillfully utilizing the media. He brought black people of all kinds from professionals to maids together in a concerted effort. For thirteen months, black Montgomery walked until finally on December 21, 1956, after a federal court order, the buses were integrated.

King later moved to Atlanta and established a headquarters for the Southern Christian Leadership Conference, a non-violent direct action group whose influence was to be felt in every corner of the South.

King was deeply influenced by the non-violent political action of Gandhi, who interestingly had been influenced by Henry David Thoreau's essay on Civil Disobedience. King fused the emotional power of the Negro church with the civil rights movement, and transformed a spontaneous racial protest into a powerful passive resistance movement with a method and an ideology. When he was criticized by a group of white southern clergy for his "unwise and untimely" demonstrations he answered in a memorable letter from the Birmingham jail. He said in part:

"I have tried to stand between two forces (in the Negro community) saying that we need not follow the 'do-nothingness' of the complacent or the hatred and despair of the black nationalist. There is a more excellent way of love and nonviolent protest. I'm grateful to God that, through the Negro church, the dimension of nonviolence entered our struggle. If this philosophy had not emerged I am convinced that by now many streets of the South would be flowing with floods of blood."

Dr. Martin Luther King, Jr. was later awarded the Nobel Prize for Peace.

Patriarchal institutions split the qualities of human nature according to sex or color—intelligence, power and rule to white males; intuition, feeling and service to blacks and to females. It is this split in the human personality which must be healed if we are to survive. Martin Luther King Jr. was able for awhile to heal that split and mobilize the inner non-violent power of diverse people.

Sometimes in recent years we have seen a regression to the old bigotry, a return to open violence against blacks, against Muslims and against whites who associate with them. A United States Senator openly expressed his nostalgic wish that a segregationist had won the presidency back in 1948. Our former President argued against the last vestiges of affirmative action in a case before the Supreme Court. And we wonder. Has anything really changed? Perhaps it has. The Senator had to step down. The Court upheld some forms of affirmative action. And perhaps the wider community will no longer give its tacit approval to acts of racial violence. When a black fraternity house was bombed at a Southern university, white students showed up to help rebuild it, to say in effect, "We do not accept or approve of such behavior." When an interracial church was bombed, white and black people in that Southern community helped the group to rebuild. And I was proud of our Unitarian Universalist congregation in Las Cruces, New Mexico when, sometime after the 9/11 catastrophe, they reached out in friendship to the local Islamic Center and invited someone to come and speak to us. Most impressive of all, we have seen an African American man sworn in as President of the United States.

When we heal that split in ourselves we begin to notice opportunities to act on our chosen values. William Ernest Hocking wrote: "To understand the times in which we live, to add our weight to the scales on the side of community and equality within valid difference, this is life with shape and character—the one eternity worth having."

Chapter 21

The Drums and Masks of Lake Geneva

When I was about ten years old, a woman from the local Methodist Church, of which my father was a member, came to visit my mother. She wanted to interest my mother in the women's group at the church and she talked at some length about the important work the women were doing, raising money to support missionary work in Africa. My mother listened and then asked, "Why would you want to do that? Don't the African people have religions of their own?"

My mother's question has stayed with me and has popped up many times over the years as I found myself living in an increasingly multi-cultural world. It came to mind recently as I looked back over the past thirty years, looking especially at the activities and accomplishments of women. There were several continent-wide Unitarian Universalist women's conferences over the years, but one stands out in my memory. It was called Womanquest and it was held at Lake Geneva in Wisconsin in 1990. About 320 Unitarian Universalist women from all over the continent were gathered to share a week of worship services, spiritual disciplines and workshops, and to draw up a vision for the future. It was the memory of that Lake Geneva conference that reminded me once again of my mother's question: Don't the African people have religions of their own?

The most striking aspect of the gathering was the pervasive use of African, Asian and European pagan spiritual disciplines. One worship service featured the African drumming and chanting that one group had chosen as their spiritual discipline for the week. Another service included a meditation of graceful Tai Chi movements by another group. The final service began with a procession of women wearing the beautifully decorated masks they had made. One evening most of the women danced a spiral dance under the stars. Songs and chants were sung with clarity and power. No mumbling or holding back. The earth and its elements were honored again and again. Those women who spoke from the pulpit, did so with a passion and spirit not often heard in our intellectual denomination.

I thought of my mother's question. And I wondered just what it was that was happening among women. We seemed to be saying, Yes, not only do other cultures have religions of their own, not only do they have important truths to teach us—not only that, but we are in fact hungering and thirsting for religious experiences no longer available in most Western religion. What is it that we needed? And why were we finding it in African drums and spiral dances?

There are at least three aspects to our need and our direction, and I would suggest that it is no accident that this phenomenon arose so powerfully in Unitarian Universalist women. Each aspect of our hunger and our journey can be related directly to one of our cherished principles. We need first and most importantly to express our whole selves as women—to celebrate our bodies, our minds and our own particular spiritual journeys. Secondly we are deeply touched by the ecological crisis of the earth and we need to rediscover ways to re-link ourselves to its cycles. And finally, we live in a world full of violence, violence between individuals and violence among nations, and we yearn for peace and safety.

Opening day at Lake Geneva comes to mind when I think of our need to celebrate ourselves as women. After registering, each woman was asked to take a long strip of brightly colored construction paper and to write her own name in the middle. Then on one end she was to write the name of a woman who was a mentor to her and on the other end the name of a woman for whom she herself was a mentor. A large hanging consisting of a long piece of driftwood with hundreds of strands of bright colored yarn dangling from it was available and each woman wove her strip of paper into the strands of yarn. The result was a colorful hanging containing the names of almost a thousand women. It was hung in the large meeting room where all the worship services took place. All week long every time I looked up at that hanging, tears welled up in my eyes as I thought of all those women whose names and lives we valued and celebrated with that simple hanging.

The second thing that seemed to me to celebrate ourselves as women was the presence of Olympia Brown's pulpit on the platform. Olympia Brown was the first woman to be ordained in this country by a recognized denomination. She was a Universalist and she served the church in Racine, Wisconsin for many years. The planning committee arranged to have her pulpit brought to the conference from Racine and at the opening service had a woman dressed as Olympia Brown speak to the gathering. All week long the pulpit was used by today's women ministers and there was something deeply moving about participating in that small piece of history.

But why did we also turn so persistently to the traditions of other cultures to celebrate ourselves as women? I think it's because the presence and power of women often seem so much more evident there than in Judaism and Christianity or even Unitarian Universalism. Patriarchy has distorted all of these traditions to one degree or another, but special ceremonies often remain to mark the life stages of women and the wisdom of the ancient mothers sometimes is still revered. In the oldest mythologies women are the givers of life and sometimes the takers of life as well. They have power! Their very bodies are held to be sacred.

Women of our dominant culture at this time in history have probably all had experiences of being overlooked and undervalued. It was exciting to see women finding special ways from around the world to celebrate our own inherent worth and dignity.

The second aspect of our need is our growing fear for the well-being of the earth. We feel caught up in a lifestyle that is destroying the planet. There are holes in the ozone layer, smog from our own cars is choking our cities, life-giving forests are disappearing. I heard on the radio that there has been a dramatic drop in the number of migrating songbirds. Governments and businesses do not respond and the damage continues. Our mainline religions have given *man* dominion over the earth as well as over women and children. We have looked upon this planet as a bundle of unlimited resources at our disposal. As women we too have been exploited. We feel for our sister, the earth. We seek a philosophy and a lifestyle that will put us back in tune with the cycles and the realities of nature. Earth religions, whether from African, Native American or Old European traditions, are based on respect for the earth and its elements. Every ritual honors the four directions, the air, the water, fire and the ground itself. Animals and rocks and rivers and trees are rightly known to be alive with energy, and worthy of respect.

We have much to learn from such traditions, and as Unitarian Universalists we are free to embrace truth wherever we find it. The women at Lake Geneva were finding in African drums and pagan dances ways to express their deep respect for the interdependent web of all existence of which we are a part.

The third aspect of our hunger is a profound yearning for an end to violence. Our lives are often measured by the wars we manage to survive. In the words of a song by Judy Small, "The first time it was fathers and the last time it was sons, and in between your husbands marched off with drums and guns."

How shall we learn to stop killing people? How shall we stop being carefully taught to hate? We have learned to believe all kinds of terrible things about whole groups of people. We have condemned the religions of other people. We have been taught that our way is the best.

As Unitarian Universalists we have a proud history of inclusiveness. We have chosen again and again to widen our identity, to walk together in more and more diversity. And during the last thirty years women have been leading the way. We are looking in depth at many traditions, searching with all our hearts for that universal impulse that we know resides in all religions. Searching until we find our woman selves in the most diverse traditions. If we can explore the spiritual disciplines of other cultures and find the universal meanings that cut across all the boundaries of race and geography and politics, will we be so quick to condemn and to kill?

I think it may be that part of our attraction to the dances and songs, the drums and masks we experienced at Lake Geneva is our deep longing to break through the many boundaries that divide us as human beings. It may be our way of moving toward that vision of a world community with peace and justice.

When the women come drumming and dancing and chanting into your life, join them! Be with us as we celebrate the inherent worth and dignity of ourselves and our foremothers as women. Join us as we express our concern for the earth and all its creatures and our respect for the interdependent web of all existence of which we are a part. Let us all learn to see ourselves in the rituals of diverse cultures, hoping to bring the world a little closer to lasting peace.

Chapter 22

Rise Up and Call Her Name

In creating *Cakes for the Queen of Heaven*, I had decided to limit the historical and archeological content to selections from the Western civilization that has come down to us—Old Europe, the Ancient Near East, Greece and Rome. It seemed to me that one brief course could not encompass all of women's religious history world-wide. Eventually of course it became clear that we needed a much wider, global view of women.

Elizabeth Fisher decided to create a course of study which would educate us about a great variety of religious traditions from around the world. Traditions which still in many ways honor woman and the earth. The course is *Rise Up and Call Her Name: A Woman-honoring Journey into Earth-based Spiritualities.*

Out of all the vivid and striking images we looked at in the process of helping Liz Fisher design this curriculum, two stand out for me. They speak to me across the boundaries of time and race and culture without even any need for explanation. One shows the terrible dark side of female history. The other envisions our hope.

At the foot of the steps of the Aztec temple in Mexico City there was found an oval stone eleven feet long, carved with the image of a dismembered goddess—Coyolxauhqui. We do not need to know her story in order to know her fate. There she lies, dismembered, for all the world to see. Is there a woman anywhere of any color or culture who does not understand and suffer with her? I believe that the message is clear and universal: with patriarchy comes the dismemberment of female power.

The other image comes from Africa—a vessel in the shape of a woman's head which has two faces. On one side a black woman's face; on the other side a white woman's face. The hair and headdresses blend into each other, telling us without words or story that we are one. I believe that such an image is the source of our hope.

I mention these two images and the meanings they hold for me because this curriculum attempts to take us on a journey into the indigenous religions of many lands and peoples and that effort is a very risky enterprise. We Unitarian Universalists are after all predominantly white middle class Americans. How dare we claim these native religions as our own? As one Native American woman said, "I feel as if you are invading my religion just as you invaded my land."

I hope we do not come to this journey as invaders. The very language of invasion speaks to me of patriarchy, not of a woman's, or a man's, spiritual journey. It is that very mind-set of invasion and conquest that we would challenge and set aside. We come to this journey as learners, as women and men who affirm, intellectually and I hope passionately, the interdependent web of all existence of which we are a part. We come now to experience directly the diversity of that web. If we are to survive we must have the courage to find and celebrate the universals at the heart of all earth-centered, woman-honoring religion.

We need to know the truth about female power and its dismemberment, and about the desacralization of the earth under patriarchy because it is part of our history as human beings. And we need to envision and celebrate our oneness even as we learn to rejoice in our colorful diversity. We do not come to invade or colonize but to re-member and to create together a new vision for the future.

In the process of writing *Cakes for the Queen of Heaven* I discovered some aspects of pre-patriarchal religion that I had not expected. Perhaps the most important was reverence for the earth and the cycles of nature. I had long been in love with the crashing waves and iridescent life of the oceans. I had stared in wonder at the beauty of the California redwoods. What I had not realized was that for the Old Religions Earth was another name for the divine female creator. I learned to sing, "We all come from the Goddess and to Her we shall return, like a drop of rain flowing to the ocean." I began to see the connection between the dishonoring of women and the exploitation of the earth. *Cakes* was about women and their lives. While we meditated upon the phases of the moon and called for harmony with earth's elements we did not take up directly the relationship between the powerlessness of women and the ecological crisis of the earth. It is exciting to me that this curriculum makes central a new respect for the earth and for women.

Another unexpected aspect of the Old Religions was ritual. As a former Episcopalian I had delighted in the absence of ritual in Unitarian Universalism. The rituals I had known earlier did not resonate with my life experience. They seemed like vain repetitions. But Sappho spoke of women dancing in the moonlight and the very title I chose for my course came from the description of a ritual for baking cakes for the Queen of Heaven. Everywhere I looked I found that ancient people created rituals. The rituals though were part of their everyday lives. I wanted *Cakes* to connect women's religious history with issues in women's lives. In trying to accomplish that goal I stumbled warily into the realm of ritual. Only a little bit of ritual—lighting a candle and reading a poem; passing a candle around the circle as each person spoke; closing each session with a poem or song. I didn't realize how starved we all were for meaningful ritual or how effective it was in touching our lives until I began to teach the course and then to hear about the rituals other women had added to the sessions. I was delighted that in this new curriculum ritual was lifted up and looked at more directly as a tool for us to use on our journey. It is a marvelous outlet for creativity.

Another aspect of pre-patriarchal religion that I bumped into in writing *Cakes* was the notion that our ancestors are still part of the community. When I decided to open the first session by having a candle passed around and each woman asked to name her female ancestors I thought it was just a way to make us aware of how few names we knew and how seldom we had an opportunity to value our mothers and grandmothers. Something else happened in the actual experience. Women spoke gently of the strengths of their mothers or the hard lives of their grandmothers. There were tears. There was laughter. Many said afterwards that they felt their mothers and grandmothers were really there with us. We had quite inadvertently called upon our ancestors, something so often done in pre-patriarchal indigenous religions that this curriculum has taken its title *Rise Up and Call Her Name* from a chant written by Carolyn McDade that is part of just such a ritual, one created by Rev. Adele Smith. In this course learning to honor our female ancestors was given its rightful emphasis and importance—another important tool for our journey.

Night and darkness also took on new meaning for me as I learned that ancient women gathered on hilltops in the light of the moon to celebrate their menses or the stages of their lives. No longer could light be all good and dark be all bad. It is no accident that in our patriarchal times we have had to call special rallies and marches in our cities to "take back the night." *Cakes* did not address this issue, and women of color rightly wondered where the goddesses of their cultures were in our very limited slice of women's religious history. This course intentionally explores the implications of our language and assumptions about light and dark as a necessary tool for this particular spiritual journey.

It was a great pleasure to me to see that these issues of respect for the earth, of ritual, of ancestors, and of darkness which were not addressed directly in *Cakes* were brought dramatically into our awareness.

The Great Goddess, that symbol of divine creativity within the world, emerges here in all her glorious colors and shapes and sounds and I would say with Luisah Teish: "I will not wear your narrow racial jackets as the blood of many nations runs sweetly thru my veins."

Chapter 23

Crete: A Partnership Conference

I climbed over the rocks and perched on the bull's horns outside the Palace of Knossos on the island of Crete. Someone took my picture and I just sat there immersed in that special moment. It was the culmination of twenty years of longing—just to be where a Goddess-centered culture had flourished for a thousand years. Here I felt a pride in my femaleness that I do not feel as easily in the religions or the politics of my own white North American culture.

I relate this very personal experience because it underlines the way in which personal religion or spirituality is inextricably bound up with the political and societal structures of our world. There I am in that moment reclaiming not only a spirituality that affirms me personally as a woman but also an extensive part of our human heritage that, according to some scholars, affirms the politics of partnership and peace. For the Minoan culture there is no evidence that women were subordinated to men, nor men to women. As far as we can tell, peace reigned for over a thousand years.

Another exciting step for me toward a multi-cultural world-view was the Partnership Conference on the island of Crete. It was organized by Riane Eisler. In her book *The Chalice and the Blade*, she called the ancient Minoan civilization of Crete an archeological "bombshell." Here was a highly developed civilization with exquisite art and buildings, a culture which at least in its early days seemed not only to have worshipped a goddess but also to have been organized in such a way that power was shared between men and women.

Eisler had presented the idea that there were two ways to structure society. One was a partnership model where power was shared. The other was a dominator model where one or more persons had power over the rest. It is this dominator model which has structured most human societies for the past three or more millennia. Eisler suggested that our early ancestors may have lived in partnership societies. These partnership cultures, like the one on Crete, were also peaceful. Archeologists could find no evidence on Crete of weapons or fortifications. Of course not all scholars agreed with Eisler's hypothesis, but it did raise an important question: What would a partnership society look like today? That was the question Eisler posed for the conference.

There were people at the conference from many countries and each participant was asked to choose one workshop to engage in for the entire conference. In a partnership society, what would families be like? Economics? Health? Education? Conflict Resolution? Art? Politics? Other workshops focused on learning more about ancient Crete, and Native American, African and other cultures.

To my surprise I was asked to work with feminist writers Carol Christ, Elinor Gadon, Naomi Goldenberg and Daniel Cohen to plan and lead the workshop on Spirituality in a partnership culture. Daniel Cohen opened some of the sessions with his new versions of old myths, told so as to present a new image of masculinity appropriate for a partnership world. Both Carol Christ and Naomi Goldenberg used the myth of Demeter and her daughter Persephone, the early version as told by Charlene Spretnak. Carol gave a moving account of her experience of her mother's death, stressing the understanding of death as part of the life cycle, the presence of love, and the need women have for myths that express the special meanings to be found in their mother-daughter relationships. Naomi stressed a view of Demeter as not only loving and grieving but also as angry and powerful, a deity able to forbid the seeds to grow and cause the land to be barren. She emphasized women's need to make use of our anger and our power as positive forces. Elinor Gadon explored the sacred female and the sacred male in other cultures, showing that the joining of male and female was celebrated as a moment of divine presence. I presented some of the global materials Elizabeth Fisher had gathered for *Rise Up and Call Her Name* about traditions that honored both women and the earth. Small group discussions, meditations, and the creation of meaningful rituals were part of each session.

On the last day of the conference participants from all the workshops gathered and each group made a brief report to all. As part of our report our group decided to close with a litany developed by participants. I believe it sums up quite eloquently our vision of spirituality in a partnership community. Rev. Mary Westfall, one of the participants in our workshop, led the entire conference in the following litany:

We Are Moving Toward Community

We seek to turn away from a spirituality that institutionalizes domination.
We are moving toward community.
We seek to turn away from a spirituality that institutionalizes exclusiveness.
We are moving toward community.
We seek to turn away from a spirituality that institutionalizes homophobia.
We are moving toward community.
We seek to turn away from a spirituality that institutionalizes racism.
We are moving toward community.
We seek to turn away from a spirituality that institutionalizes violence.
We are moving toward community.
As we seek to turn away from oppressive forms of spirituality, we seek a partnership way.
We affirm a spirituality that celebrates diversity.
We are moving toward community.
We affirm a spirituality that celebrates the sacredness of life, the sacredness of earth, the sacredness of sexuality.
We are moving toward community.
We affirm a spirituality that celebrates expressions of the divine: sacred male, sacred female, sacred cosmos.
We are moving toward community.

We affirm a spirituality that is grounded in personal experience,
and values the spiritual journey of each person.
We are moving toward community.
We affirm a spirituality that celebrates individuality and the
interconnectedness of all things.
We are moving toward community.
We affirm a spirituality that leads us into deeper experience of
community.
We are moving toward community.

from SHIRLEY'S CAULDRON

Spring makes me think of ferries. I love ferries. Whenever I go to San Francisco I take the ferry from Larkspur Landing. I enjoy not only that ferry ride—sunshine on the water, cool breezes and views of the city and its bridges—but all the ferry rides of the past as well.

For awhile when I was a child we lived in Weehawken, up on the palisades across the Hudson River from New York City. My father took the ferry to work each day, and sometimes on Saturday he would take me with him. We walked down some 300 steps to the big old ferry, yellow and grimy, at the bottom of the palisades. On board we bought coffee and doughnuts and got our shoes shined. I always liked to be outside where I could watch the waves we made and the birds circling overhead. I don't seem to have any memory of walking back up the 300 steps on the way home.

Those commuter ferries were discontinued many years ago, but on my last visit to New Jersey I was delighted to find that there is a new small gleaming white ferry that takes shoppers from Weehawken to midtown Manhattan. The old steps are still there but fenced off and there is a parking lot at the foot of the palisades.

A couple of times in my life I visited Bermuda and rode the ferries there, amazed that children rode the ferries to and from school. And there was a quaint little ferry that held three cars, somewhere on the border between Spain and Portugal. When I lived in Mobile, Alabama I rode another small ferry between Dauphin Island and Fort Morgan. And then in the Seattle area I enjoyed the huge ferries that cris-cross Puget Sound, and on days when "the mountains are out" give you one of the most dramatic mountain and water views anywhere.

Ferries take me places in a steady, unhurried way so I enjoy the journey as much as the destination. The journey is home, as my old friend and mentor, Nelle Morton, so cleverly said.

Blessed be!

SPIRAL SIX

Offerings to Hecate

We must confess that we are the possible
We are the miraculous,
we are the true wonder of this world
That is when, and only when,
We come to it.

-Maya Angelou

Chapter 24

Crones

In her beautiful telling of the myth of the Goddess Hecate, Charlene Spretnak writes: ". . . they offered Her ritual suppers at lonely crossroads . . . When Hecate's rites were observed, the black nights passed silently one into another. But if the Goddess was defied, She unleashed the power of Her wrath and swept over the earth, bringing storms and destruction."

Hecate. Do you know Her? She is old and wise and very powerful. Firmly She stirs the bubbling cauldron of life and death. She has been ignored and almost forgotten for many centuries. She has been ridiculed, called ugly and hideous and dangerous whenever She has appeared. She has certainly been defied. But today Her power is rising. She represents the power, the wisdom and the wrath of old women and our numbers are increasing at a phenomenal rate. Hecate is the Crone within each of us. Will we seize the opportunities before us and accept the challenge of Hecate's crossroads?

As we observe the three thea/ological imperatives or spirals which have emerged as we face the future, what roads have we traveled in order to implement the feminist imperative, the scientific-environmental imperative, and the multi-cultural imperative? We need to remember that these imperatives are interconnected in complex ways. It is almost impossible to speak or write of them separately.

Hecate reminds us of the sacred history that is ours as women. Hecate reminds us that divine power, the power of life and death, was for many thousands of years thought to be female. In recent decades, using *Cakes for the Queen of Heaven* and other courses, women have studied and reclaimed our pre-patriarchal religious history where women were revered. Myths tell us that in very early times the Goddess reigned, and sociologists tell us that the myths of a culture reflect its social arrangements. Women must have had power and respect. Later myths tell us that male deities waged battles against the Goddess and that male deities were exalted to the most powerful positions. But the Goddesses were still there. Mythology tells us that in early historic times Goddesses and Gods reigned together with varying amounts of power. Reclaiming that heritage empowered many women to recognize more fully their own inherent worth and dignity.

Other women have held up to light the strong women within Judaism and Christianity who stood on thresholds between old traditions which honored women and newer ones which were taking away that respect, women who struggled to retain some power for women. Biblical scholar Savina Teubal suggests that the matriarchs of Genesis—Sarah, Rebecca and Rachel—were priestesses of an old Mesopotamian religion struggling to maintain customs of matrilineal descent and powerful female influence at a time and in a place where the newer patriarchal ways were taking over.

Scholar Elaine Pagels suggests that Mary Magdalene was believed by the early Gnostic Christians to be not only a full-fledged Apostle but a leader among the Apostles. We did not know about her as an apostle until recently because the church fathers of the fourth century, when deciding which writings to include in the official canon, had pronounced the Gnostic writings to be heresy. All the writings that mentioned Mary Magdalene unanimously pictured her as one of Jesus' most trusted disciples. All were excluded from the New Testament canon, and as Pagels points out, "When these texts came to be excluded . . . many Christians excluded as well the conviction that women could—and should—participate in leading the churches."

Rev. Kendyl Gibbons lifted up another historical record one year at the UU General Assembly. Wearing a jeweled crown, she stepped up to the podium and impersonated 16th century Queen Isabella of Transylvania. She told the story of how *she* came to issue the first known Edict of Religious Toleration—on behalf of her young son who reconfirmed the edict when he became king. Until Rev. Gibbons' presentation, the young king had usually received credit for the famous edict. Looking at more recent history, historian Cynthia Grant Tucker documented in *Prophetic Sisterhood* the work of the 19th century women ministers who founded and served Unitarian churches on the mid-western frontier. More recently in *No Silent Witness: The*

Eliot Parsonage Women and Their Unitarian World Tucker explored the contributions of eight women of the distinguished Eliot family of Unitarians. Thus the voices of important lay women were brought to light. Women scholars in religion as in every field have been researching the lives of brilliant and important women.

African American women scholars have developed a body of research that explores their particular religious history. Many define themselves and their work as "womanist" rather than "feminist." Others prefer to call themselves black feminists. Womanist is a term coined by poet Alice Walker in her book *In Search of Our Mothers' Gardens: Womanist Prose*. Part of her definition is as follows: From womanish. (Opp. of "girlish," i.e., frivolous, irresponsible, not serious.) A black feminist or feminist of color. From the black folk expression of mothers of female children, "You acting womanish," i.e., like a woman. Usually referring to outrageous, audacious, courageous or willful behavior. Wanting to know more and in greater depth than is considered "good" for one. Interested in grown-up doings. Acting grown up. Being grown up. Interchangeable with another black folk expression: "You trying to be grown." Responsible. In charge. Serious . . . . Womanist is to feminist as purple is to lavender.

Arisika Razak, who says of herself, "I am not a Christian, but I am an activist and healer," embraces Walker's definition of womanist. She writes, "For me, the struggles for racial justice, women's rights, and the right to love whomever I wish—of whatever race or gender I choose—along with my freedom to worship the sacred as I know, name, and experience it, come together in a weave that honors my slave and free ancestors of African lineage, my Euro-American and indigenous roots, and my love and respect for the healing powers of the earth. For me, this holistic tapestry of liberation is best named by the term womanist, a term that is feminist, Afrocentric, healing, embodied, and spiritual."

Hecate also reminds us of our connection with the earth, the storms and destruction as well as the beauty, death as part of the cycle of life.

Women scholars and thealogians have begun the process of changing the myths and symbols which support our social structures. Starhawk and Luisah Teish have reclaimed ancient European and African pagan traditions which honor not only women but also the earth, and in the process have created new religions and new stories for the modern world. Others, like Sophia Fahs and Carol Christ have looked not only to the ancient past or to other cultures for understanding and inspiration, but also to the wonders of our own modern philosophies and sciences, sources which seem to suggest the immanence of the divine and the interconnectedness of the cosmos. Feminists everywhere are celebrating "the interdependent web of all existence of which we are a part."

Philosopher-scientist Elisabet Sahtouris has raised another interesting question: "What if modern science and our view of human society had evolved from organic biology rather than from mechanical physics?" Our heritage has been to see ourselves as separate from the rest of nature rather than as living beings within a larger living being—the earth. As the old mechanical worldview gave way to an organic view, we have had to take a new look at evolution. We find that cooperation rather than competition has made the emergence of new and more complex organisms possible. Perhaps humanity can once more learn to resolve conflicts and to live in harmony with the rest of nature by means of cooperation instead of competition.

Many feminists have been troubled, as I was, by the psychologically unhealthy ethic of self-sacrifice which pervades Western tradition. Sophia Fahs was one of the first to point out that while some beliefs are healthy, other beliefs are downright unhealthy. In *It Matters What We Believe*, she wrote: "Some beliefs weaken a person's selfhood. They blight the growth of resourcefulness. Other beliefs nurture self-confidence and enrich the feeling of personal worth."

Mary Daly pointed out years ago that an ethic of self-sacrifice is especially oppressive to women who are excluded from power but called to an ethic of martyrdom. Rita Nakashima Brock and Rebecca Ann Parker were also troubled by the ethic of self-sacrifice which "uses Jesus' death as the supreme model of self-sacrificing love, placing victims in harm's way and absolving perpetrators of their responsibility for unethical behavior." Their research on early Christianity surprisingly suggests that images of Jesus' crucifixion did not appear in churches until the tenth century. Until then the Christian Church had emphasized and celebrated earthly paradise as the expression of divine love. In the second millennium of the Christian era, however, "A new age began—one in which the execution of Jesus would become a sacrifice to be repeated first on the Eucharistic altar and then in the ravages of a full-blown holy war."

Feminist thea/ologian Sharon Welch has also rejected the martyr ethic saying, "Self-sacrifice is an inadequate model of love even for those who are members of the dominant strata of society . . . Solidarity does not require self-sacrifice but an enlargement of the self to include community with others. To work with others is not to lose oneself, but first and foremost, it is to find a larger self." She proposes instead an ethic of risk, the risks of relationship. She offers the analogy of jazz, saying, "Jazz emerges from the interplay of structure and improvisation, collectivity and individuality, tradition and innovation . . . The pleasure and energy of jazz comes from hearing both a familiar chord progression and melody and the new possibilities, what can be done from that structure . . . the technical skill and creativity of each player is as foundational as is the spark that comes from playing off of each other." Of our communities and our work for social justice she writes: "As we listen to each other, as we are open to seeing and playing off our limits and strengths, weaknesses and possibilities, what happens with all of our strategies, our coalitions, our communities, even our work for justice? It swings!"

Thandeka and others have spoken out for the importance of an embedded thea/ology of small group ministry for the development of relationships of depth. Feminist spirituality groups have helped many women build relationships of honesty and depth. Many of our congregations now have small groups which seem to function much as that Parents Without Partners group did for Eeyore.

In courses such as *Rise Up and Call Her Name* and in international conferences women have begun a serious multi-cultural dialogue about our personal lives and our deepest values. Engaging in more than dialogue, women are organizing around the world to improve women's health, education and political and financial power. Patriarchal societies are slowly learning that when women's lives are improved the whole community benefits. I believe that what makes that work not only possible but exciting is our growing reverence for the relationships we experience in this life even in the face of destruction and cruelty.

In our women's groups and in our congregations we have begun to celebrate ourselves and our relationships and to find ways to honor the earth. We are learning to honor our bodies and the earth as the location of the sacred, and to walk together with more and more diverse people in our quest for peace and justice.

Unitarian Universalists and women involved in feminist spirituality are often troubled by our difficulty in explaining to friends from diverse traditions who we are or what we believe. Some Unitarian Universalists have even developed short "elevator speeches" so that they can respond briefly without looking or feeling too foolish. I am reminded of serving as minister at the UU Fellowship in Mobile, Alabama. When one of our members decided to run for mayor of the city, the Fellowship phone began to ring repeatedly every day. Religion was apparently very important to the voters; the callers all wanted to know, "What do Unitarian Universalists believe?" I had no elevator speech. I kept a copy of our UU principles next to the phone and said to everyone who called, "We don't have a creed, but we do have a set of principles and they are . . ." I would then start reading the principles. After hearing two or three the caller would say, "Oh. OK. Thank you." And hang up. They seemed satisfied and our member, Mike Dow, won the election—to the surprise and delight of the UU Fellowship.

Faced with a growing ethnic and thea/ological diversity in our society and in our congregations UUs often wondered what kind of thea/ology could possibly hold us all together. During the first decade of this new century delegates to our General Assembly elected a Commission of nine people to explore this question. They produced a book titled *Engaging Our Theological Diversity*.

They reported that there is wide consensus among UUs that our liberal message is important in this troubled world, but that we have difficulty articulating that message. The authors wonder: Is our thea/ological diversity getting in the way, or have we just not done the difficult work necessary to find our common ground and give it voice?

I have to admit that I was troubled by the demand for some central belief we could all cling to, something I feared would allow us to draw a firm boundary line between us and "them," those strangers outside. UU feminist thea/ologian Sharon Welch expresses a similar concern. She writes: "What bothers me about the calls for common ground is that this very concept of community is predicated upon denying what I see as the richness of community, a richness created as much by difference and surprise as by similarity and affirmation."

I love our diversity and I have felt that our seven principles were enough glue to hold us together. And yet I too have felt the need to articulate our UU identity in new and ever more inclusive terms.

Part of our problem with *theology* is the word itself. The Greek roots mean the study of a male God. Even if we change the spelling to *thealogy*, the study of a Goddess, we don't find that topic very interesting because most of us don't believe in a supernatural deity anyway. At most we may use the term to sum up our highest ideals of justice and love, or to acknowledge the wonder and mystery of the universe. For women however the change in spelling can at least serve to acknowledge our pre-patriarchal heritage when the divine was indeed imaged as female. I like Carol Christ's term *thea/ology*, both female and male roots used to designate not a supernatural being or realm but rather the creative potential within this world. I see the term more as an acknowledgement of our past, pre-patriarchal and patriarchal. For me Tillich's *ultimate reality* or *ground of being* work better for the present and future. Classical systematic theology is really about the existential questions we all face as human beings: Who am I? How do I know what I know? What is my relationship to the universe? What is my relationship to other people? In the past, and for some people today, the male God is brought in to provide the answers.

The writers of *Engaging Our Theological Diversity* rightly focused upon the questions and how we in the 21st century tend to answer them. They met with hundreds of UUs from all over the country, collected survey data from hundreds more, and studied our history as Unitarians, as Universalists and as Unitarian Universalists. The vision that emerges, expressed in twelve statements, is I think not essentially different from our principles. It is a powerful vision, and one that can be claimed by all strands of the UU tradition.

I was especially struck by and agree with two particular quotations in the book. I believe they are crucial in understanding what has changed in UU thea/ology during the past thirty years. The first is by David Bumbaugh. He suggests that our seventh principle is central to a faith for the twenty-first century. He writes: "The seventh Principle calls us to reverence before the world, not some future world, but this miraculous world of our everyday experience. It challenges us to understand the world as reflexive and relational rather than hierarchical. It bespeaks a world in which neither god nor humanity is at the center, in which the center is the void, the ever fecund matrix out of which being emerges."

And Charlotte Shivvers writes: "The very emptiness that is left in that central place is neither weakness nor failure. It can become a place of humility, acceptance, and wonder—and a place where we all can meet."

In looking back over this recent history however, I find I have a rather large bone to pick with this book. I like the vision that the writers suggest, but I feel that once again the contributions of women have been overlooked and undervalued. For women especially some very practical, tangible changes have taken place in Unitarian Universalism—a great increase in the number of women ministers, and both a hymnal and a principles document revised so as to be almost free of sexist language. The exception of course is the continued use of the male "God" to designate the divine. Not using male pronouns or adjectives for God is supposed to de-genderize the term but it doesn't really. It is just one more use of the male term for the generic. These are, however, giant changes, but only one is mentioned in the book—the increase in the number of women ministers—and nothing is said about how these changes came about.

The Women & Religion Resolution of 1977 is very briefly mentioned in the book. It is not quoted and the description of it as "aimed at bringing a set of values to the center of our religious faith and practice: relationship, equity and justice, inclusiveness, open process, compassion, and focus on family and children." makes it sound "nice" (remember my father's comment about that word?) something like a sweet affirmation of our principles with a little added focus on "family and children." The actual resolution used strong language. It spoke of women being overlooked and undervalued It demanded that we examine our theologies, our organizational structure and our language so as to root out sexism. And that's how we got the revised hymnal and principles and the huge increase in the number of women ministers.

Women put our chairs into circles and created new more personal worship like the Candles of Joy and Concern and the Water Ceremony. In the Commission's book these innovations are mentioned but nothing is said about where they came from.

Women celebrated the inherent worth and dignity of ourselves and our foremothers by bringing women's history and writings and music into our worship. Only one song, Spirit of Life, is mentioned in the book as "by far the most commonly sung UU song," even called the "standard UU anthem." The composer, Carolyn McDade is not mentioned whereas every contribution by a man is credited by name. The book does not mention that in the old 1964 hymnal only 26 of the 327 songs had words or music written by women, and only one reading out of 231 was written by a woman. Or that in the later 1993 hymnal 71 out of 415 of the songs have words or music written by women, and that 83 out of 318 readings are written by women. Big changes in 29 years, as well as a long way yet to go. It has been my impression too that in the later hymnal our contemporary song writers, both female and male have long been articulating our thea/ology with considerable clarity. I think of Shelley Jackson Denham's *We Laugh, We Cry*, Jim Scott's *Gather the Spirit*, Kendyl Gibbons' *Lady of the Season's Laughter* (music by David Hurd), to name but a few.

Women like Sophia Fahs first rediscovered our sacred connection to the web of life, and later women were leaders in advocating for the seventh principle. This principle is celebrated in the book as a radical and vital shift in thea/ology, but Fahs and the other women are not mentioned.

Women, hoping to bring the world a little closer to lasting peace, were the first to learn to see ourselves in the rituals of diverse indigenous cultures which still retain some pre-patriarchal respect for women and the earth, opening our minds and hearts to the very diversity that gave rise to the book. But the book does not acknowledge the primary role of women in creating this new vision for thea/ology.

Even with the powerful vision presented by the Commission, we still struggle to articulate a faith that can unite us even as it encompasses our diversity. In a recent article in the *UU World* magazine, David Bumbaugh complains that "the effort to restate the faith tradition in light of contemporary challenges has been swept away by the fear . . . that if we define ourselves too clearly, someone may be offended." My own related concern, as a Unitarian Universalist and as a feminist, is that we not lapse into sentimentality, romanticizing women, nature and diverse traditions as we try to be inclusive.

Betty Roszak makes a similar point about romanticizing women and nature. She writes: "But the crucial question has to be raised. Are women once more to be identified with the archetypal mother, or Mother Nature? . . . Or is this just another repetition of the old stereotyping we have tried so hard to break?"

The reasons for our difficulty in saying what we believe are as complex as the diversity we seek, but I do think that we could do better than elevator speeches. Indeed Bumbaugh himself has made an impressive attempt to say what Unitarian Universalists believe even as we become more and more inclusive of many paths. He writes:

"We believe that the universe in which we live and move and have our being is the expression of an inexorable process that began in eons past, ages beyond our comprehension and has evolved from singularity to multiplicity, from simplicity to complexity, from disorder to order.

We believe that the earth and all who live upon the earth are products of the same process that swirled the galaxies into being, that ignited the stars and orbited the planets through the night sky, that we are expressions of that universal process which has created and formed us out of recycled star dust.

We believe that all living things are members of a single community, all expressions of a planetary process that produced life and sustains it in intricate ways beyond our knowing. We hold the life process itself to be sacred.

We believe that the health of the human venture is inextricably dependent upon the integrity of the rest of the community of living things and upon the integrity of those processes by which life is bodied forth and sustained. Therefore we affirm that we are called to serve the planetary process upon which life depends.

We believe that in this interconnected existence the well-being of one cannot be separated from the well-being of the whole, that ultimately we all spring from the same source and all journey to the same ultimate destiny.

We believe that the universe outside of us and the universe within us is one universe. Because that is so, our efforts, our dreams, our hopes, our ambitions are the dreams, hopes and ambitions of the universe itself. In us, and perhaps elsewhere, the Universe is reaching toward self-awareness, toward self-consciousness.

We believe that our efforts to understand the world and our place within it are an expression of the universe's deep drive toward meaning. In us, and perhaps elsewhere, the Universe dreams dreams and reaches toward unknown possibilities. We hold as sacred the unquenchable drive to know and to understand.

We believe that the moral impulse that weaves its way through our lives, luring us to practices of justice and mercy and compassion, is threaded through the universe itself and it is this universal longing that finds outlet in our best moments.

We believe that our location within the community of living things places upon us inescapable responsibilities. Life is more than our understanding of it, but the level of our comprehension demands that we act out of conscious concern for the broadest vision of community we can command and that we seek not our welfare alone, but the welfare of the whole. We are commanded to serve life and serve it to the seven times seventieth generation.

We believe that those least like us, those located on the margins have important contributions to make to the rest of the community of life and that in some curious way, we are all located on the margins.

We believe that all that functions to divide us from each other and from the community of living things is to be resisted in the name of that larger vision of a world everywhere alive, everywhere seeking to incarnate a deep, implicate process that called us into being, that sustains us in being, that transforms us as we cannot transform ourselves, that receives us back to itself when life has used us up. Not knowing the end of that process, nonetheless we trust it, we rest in it, and we serve it."

I would not like to see us try to impose a set of beliefs on all UUs. However, I like his statement, except for a few phrases such as "We serve" and "We are commanded" which I think perpetuate authoritarian patriarchal attitudes of the past. I would prefer to say "We choose," and "We are committed." The statement is nevertheless an excellent description of the world-view which has emerged from today's sciences and philosophies and how we humans can best find meaning and responsibility within that world-view. It may well be the world-view that Troelstch thought would be necessary for a religion such as ours.

Our quest for diversity challenges us to seek out and celebrate the positive aspects of many traditions even as we resist injustice wherever found. Rebecca Parker suggests that within our diversity we do have a "defining focus" which is "a devotion to the flourishing of life." The rest of her statement seems not only to echo our UU Principles and Purposes and the vision produced by the authors of *Engaging Our Theological Diversity* but also to be similar to the statement by David Bumbaugh. She writes: "People of progressive faith care for the sacredness of this world, this life, here and now. We do not look to a world to come that will be more valuable than this world. We cherish our bodies, this earth, this time and place that is within our grasp. We reverence the intimate, intricate, and unshakeable reality that all life is connected. We honor and respect the bonds that tie each to all, that weave us into an inescapable net of mutuality. We vow to care for the interdependent web of existence; we desire all life to thrive, and therefore we resist those social evils and systemic injustices that benefit a few at the expense of many, or that allow a privileged existence for some while others have their hearts and bodies broken by exploitation, prejudice, censure, or lack of access to the rights and resources needed for life. We critique any conception of God that functions to bless an unjust status quo or to alleviate human responsibility. We affirm a covenant among all beings that we honor with our hearts, souls, mind, and strength. We will do everything in our power to assure that this covenant of life, for life, is honored. And we seek to connect our circle with other circles of life, to expand our circle into ever-widening ripples of influence for good."

I believe our quest is founded upon a serious covenant we have with each other as Unitarian Universalists and I hope as feminists: to respect the freedom of each person to find her own spiritual path and to understand that there are many valid ways to express our positive human potential.

While at the Graduate Theological Union, I took a course entitled "The Status of Women in the Old Testament." The professor was very distinguished. The class was a small seminar. During one class session the professor was struggling valiantly and with much erudition to justify the presence of a particularly brutal (to women) story in the canon and to give it some positive meaning for women. I asked him why we couldn't just ignore or reject such stories and focus on whatever positive content there might be for women elsewhere in the scriptures. He looked surprised and said, "Why, because the entire canon is authoritative for the community of faith." Not my community of faith, I thought to myself, and in that moment I knew that Unitarian Universalism had something very special to offer to women: the freedom to reject religious writings, symbols and teachings which do not resonate with *female* experience, and the freedom to seek out and affirm religious writings, symbols and teachings which *women* find meaningful. We have faith in our human freedom to choose what we find of value in any religious or secular writings.

To claim such freedom of choice means that we look to no authority but that of our own experience. Each person is forced back upon her own personal and community experience with the divine as the final authority for what is loving or just. The divine is experienced as immanent in oneself, in one's community and in the natural world. We can be open to the use of a variety of religious myths and symbols if we believe that the truth expressed by any one tradition is partial.

Over the years the booths in the exhibit hall at General Assembly have gradually become like a manifestation of this freedom covenant. One early year the Christian Fellowship had its booth directly opposite the booth for the Covenant of Unitarian Universalist Pagans. I sat there one day and watched as one person after another came down the aisle, looked at the two booths and burst out laughing. Often they stopped to talk with the people in both booths, rejoicing in that freedom. Now everyone takes for granted the presence not only of these two groups but many others as well—UUs for Jewish Awareness, the Buddhist Fellowship, UU Mystics, UU Humanists, and so on. We believe in that freedom covenant and we are learning to make it work. The dramatic proliferation of these many paths within Unitarian Universalism in recent years should be recognized as an important source of our continuing growth. That covenant has meant a great deal to me as a woman, even as I recognize the need for a world-view, a clear statement of how we view the universe, to go with it. I think we know very well who we are as Unitarian Universalists and that both our world-view and our mission in life are implied, if not stated, in our

Principles and Purposes document. I believe our world-view is stated most explicitly in David Bumbaugh's statement quoted above, and our mission or purpose most explicitly in Rebecca Parker's statement quoted above. These statements may also appeal to many feminists, both within and outside of Unitarian Universalism.

Chapter 25

Crossroads Old and New

Hecate reminds us that we are always meeting at some new cross-roads. The myth in that sense suggests what we now say is scientifically true: that our world is constantly changing and that we are repeatedly faced with choices as to how we will respond. In the past we have chosen many roads and left others unexplored. Every choice has led to unexpected, unpredictable consequences. One consequence was that because of ancient conquests and choices regarding power, we failed to honor and to tell the female half of our story. Women today are reclaiming that part of our heritage.

Another consequence of past choices was our tendency to believe that some groups of people were superior to others. Racism still haunts us but women of color are doing their own research and asserting their own special identities.

One of the most destructive choices made in the past was to treat the earth and our whole earthly life as fallen and sinful. In letting go of a belief in a supernatural realm, we have had to realize that if there is divinity anywhere it is right here in the beauties of our material world, in our own bodies, in our relationships with each other and with the daffodils. I have long experienced a sense of awe and amazement at the wonders of love and birth, the stunning beauty of the ocean and flowers and snow-capped mountains—the vastness of the universe on the one hand and the incredible microscopic intricacy of life on the other. I choose to celebrate all of that. I do not however choose to follow the suggestion that we call this creativity of the universe *God*. The word *god* carries the patriarchal assumption of maleness. It is not gender-neutral. To most people the word also carries the assumption of some supernatural being or power. I prefer to live with mystery rather than cling to the language and assumptions of the past.

Process thought has helped me to understand my world in all its indeterminacy and novelty. No wonder we celebrate what seems reliable in the natural world—solstices, phases of the moon, the rising and setting of the sun. We know we suffer, we know we change and will die. And yet we celebrate what is beautiful and reliable. We know there is destruction and cruelty in ourselves as well as in others, and yet we dare to love and care.

Many thea/ologians and psychologists have struggled with the paradox of love and cruelty. What seems possible to me is that the cosmos, the earth, and we humans all contain a range of potential from positive constructive events or behavior to negative destructive events or behavior. We are like the proverbial snowflake, each one subject to all the chance variables of the original ice plus the wind, humidity, and temperature as we float down, and thus are not only infinite in our differences but also changing and growing in our understandings. Forsaking the rigid determinism and reductionism of past philosophies, we seem to have some freedom to make choices even as we are subject to the chance happenings of the universe.

We could continue to make more and more lethal weapons until we destroy the planet. Or the earth could be struck by a giant asteroid. We could choose to move toward more and more community and cooperation. And chance may favor the continued existence of a beautiful earth for us to enjoy. We stand once more at Hecate's crossroads. Which road will we take? In such a world the answer my friend is still "blowin' in the wind." Sharon Welch suggests that "Our goal is neither the ultimate defeat of evil nor fundamental and permanent social change. It is simply (but significantly) a less destructive way of playing who and what we are. For this we need new transformative metaphors for compassionate, self-critical, and creative engagement." I think we do have some clues—some metaphors and symbols that may help us in our choices and in our relationship to our world.

When women came together to study our own history and to share our personal experiences with each other, we were not just studying the past. We were evolving a whole new world-view and thea/ology for the future. One of the most important things we learned was that in ancient Turkey and in Old Europe and on the island of Crete, no evidence of weapons or fortifications can be found in the earliest stages of human civilization. Carol Lee Flinders suggests that at the earliest stages of human civilization, survival of the group depended upon a social order of cooperation. According to Barbara G. Walker, "There is no doubt that the Goddess image has induced more tolerant, peaceful, kind, and caring societies than the god image, whose societies always tended toward war, violence, puritanism, and hierarchy." Whether or not we agree with these findings and interpretations, they do raise a huge question for us about the future. The Goddess image has emerged powerfully in our own day. After some 5000 years of patriarchal competition, hatred and vicious wars, we have developed more and more lethal weapons which can destroy not only ourselves but the entire planet. Not to mention the growing problems of pollution and global warming. We need to stop and to ask ourselves if we still know how to establish a social order based upon cooperation and the absence of weapons and fortifications. We need to ask what new story, symbol or world-view would reflect and support such a society.

The root metaphor of patriarchal traditions is dominance-submission, master-slave, and women have been the most universal slaves. The sanctuaries of patriarchal religion are designed to reinforce the metaphor. A dominant male perched high in a pulpit hands down the "word" of the male god to the submissive supplicants below. It matters little what the "word" is; it is the behavior that teaches most powerfully. The combination of arrogance above and seething resentment below engendered by this behavioral metaphor has brought us to the brink of disaster.

A religion or thea/ology of the future must have a new root metaphor. Perhaps it should be that web of intricate interconnections. We can begin to live a new metaphor and to articulate a new ethic as Sharon Welch has done. We need no longer be caught between arrogance and sacrifice. We can arrange our sanctuaries so that they reinforce our connectedness, our respect for each other's personal authority and inner journeys whether male or female. We can come down from our pulpits; we can learn from each other. We can use language that includes women as well as men. We can use symbols that point toward the ultimate reality of our own material world. We can honor as a large part of our human heritage the pre-patriarchal religions in which female deities were revered. We can do all of these things if we are open to the insights of many stories, symbols and forms of celebration.

There may however be some powerful universal symbols to carry us into the future. When I was invited to do my odyssey or spiritual autobiography for my ministerial colleagues a few years ago, I brought along a coffee cup and a cocktail glass—to represent my early life—and my small chalice that I use for workshops. My parents always had a lot of company and when friends arrived the typical greeting in the day time was "Come on in and have a cup of coffee!" or in the evening "Come on in and have a drink!" As I placed the cup, the glass and the chalice on the table to begin my odyssey, I was aware once again of what a universal symbol the cup or chalice is. It has been central in ancient pagan rituals and in many religious traditions around the world. Most importantly, it is an everyday experience of welcome. It is both old and new, both personal and universal. Perhaps it will help us move further toward community.

Another symbol of the emerging world view might be that photo of the earth taken from space. Such a photo expresses in one stunning image the wonders of our modern science and technology and the wholeness and beauty of our ancient home. From space the planet looks like a giant living organism. Some have called it a goddess. As a symbol it resonates on many levels. It is always moving and changing. Even before this image was available to us, philosopher-scientists were already suggesting that our world is not static, put in place all at once. It is instead an ongoing process of change and novelty, and there it is before our eyes, our shifting, swirling "blue boat home." The image also has a wholeness or oneness which comes as both a shock and a message of hope to us as we struggle with the divisions and hatreds among us. Seeing the total organism of which we are a part, we may begin to feel a certain kinship with all the life of our planet. At yet another level the grandeur of the image may cause us to wonder why we have denigrated and destroyed so much of this amazing organism. Why have we equated this world, our world, even our own earthly bodies with evil? Finally, the image expands our world-view to a cosmic awareness unknown to past generations. The vastness of space-time surrounds us, and may lead us again to a feeling of closeness with all of life.

And finally there is the spiral, the shape and structure of our DNA, our galaxy, our universe. A symbol which reminds us of our past, our present and the unknown possibilities of our future.

As we work to create new spirals on our journey, let us heed these words by Jane Caputi: "Imagine the Crones standing over a raging fire in the dead of night. Hanging above that dragon fire is a giant cauldron that changes colors from purple to silver to copper to red and finally to black. The Crones are waving large, crooked sticks over its surface, stirring up trouble, brewing up brainstorms, reconstituting creation. The cauldron is the magical matrix of Chaos into which all the structures by which we have been ruled and controlled for millennia are now crackling, cracking, and dissolving. Peer with your owl eyes into the rising, infinitely turbulent steam. Become fateful, taking responsibility for what turn our world is now taking."

Appendix
Unitarian Universalist Principles

We, the member congregations of the Unitarian Universalist Association, covenant to affirm and promote:

The inherent worth and dignity of every person
Justice, equity and compassion in human relations
Acceptance of one another and encouragement to spiritual growth in our congregations
A free and responsible search for truth and meaning
The right of conscience and the use of the democratic process within our congregations and in society at large
The goal of world community with peace, liberty, and justice for all
Respect for the interdependent web of all existence of which we are a part.

Women and Religion Resolution of 1977

WHEREAS, a principle of the Unitarian Universalist Association is to "affirm, defend, and promote the supreme worth and dignity of every human personality, and the use of the democratic method in human relationships;" and

WHEREAS, great strides have been taken to affirm this principle within our denomination; and

WHEREAS, some models of human relationships arising from religious myths, historical materials, and other teachings still create and perpetuate attitudes that cause women everywhere to be overlooked and undervalued; and

WHEREAS, children, youth and adults internalize and act on these cultural models, thereby tending to limit their sense of self-worth and dignity;

THEREFORE, BE IT RESOLVED: That the 1977 General Assembly of the Unitarian Universalist Association calls upon all Unitarian Universalists to examine carefully their own religious beliefs and the extent to which these beliefs influence sex-role stereotypes within their own families; and

BE IT FURTHER RESOLVED: That the General Assembly urges the Board of Trustees of the Unitarian Universalist Association to encourage the Unitarian Universalist Association administrative officers and staff, the religious leaders within societies, the Unitarian Universalist theological schools, the directors of related organizations, and the planners of seminars and conferences, to make every effort to: (a) put traditional assumptions and language in perspective, and (b) avoid sexist assumptions and language in the future.

BE IT FURTHER RESOLVED: That the General Assembly urges the President of the Unitarian Universalist Association to send copies of this resolution to other denominations examining sexism inherent in religious literature and institutions and to the International Association of Liberal Religious Women and the International Association for Religious Freedom; and

BE IT FURTHER RESOLVED: That the General Assembly requests the Unitarian Universalist Association (a) to join with those who are encouraging others in the society to examine the relationship between religious and cultural attitudes toward women, and (b) to send a representative and resource materials to associations appropriate to furthering the above goals; and

BE IT FURTHER RESOLVED: That the General Assembly requests the President of the UUA to report annually on progress in implementing this resolution.

~ The above resolution was passed unanimously. Ithaca, NY 1977

References

Angelou, Maya, *A Brave and Startling Truth*, New York: Random House, 1995.

Bachofen, Jacob. *Myth, Religion and Mother Right,* Bollingen series LXXIV, Princeton University Press, 1967.

Barbour, Ian G. *Issues in Science and Religion*, New York: Harper & Row, 1966.

Baughan, Raymond, "Sounds of Silence," in *Great Occasions*, Carl Seaburg (ed.) Boston: Skinner House Books, Unitarian Universalist Association, 1988, p. 135.

Bennett, Lerone *Before the Mayflower: a History of Black America*, Chicago: Johnson Publishing Co., 2003.

Beuhrens, John and Parker, Rebecca. *A House for Hope*, Boston: Beacon Press, 2010.

Bevan, W. "The Sound of the Wind That's Blowing," *American Psychologist*, 31, 1976, pp. 481-491.

"Blue Boat Home," in *Singing the Journey*, Boston: Unitarian Universalist Association, 2005, #1064.

Bumbaugh, David in *CUUPS Bulletin,* July 2008.

_____ "The Unfulfilled Promise," *UU World*, Summer 2011, p. 34.

Campbell, Joseph. *The Masks of God: Primitive Mythology*, NY: Viking Penguin, Inc. 1976.

Caputi, Jane. *Gossips, Gorgons and Crones*, Santa Fe NM: Bear & Company, 1993.

Christ, Carol P. *She Who Changes: Re-imagining the Divine in the World*, New York: Palgrave Macmillan, 2003.

cummings, ee, *Complete Poems,* George J. Firmage (ed.), New York: Liveright, 1991.

Daly, Mary. *Beyond God the Father*, Boston: Beacon Press, 1973.

Denham, Shelley Jackson, in *Singing the Living Tradition*, Boston: Beacon Press, 1993, #354.

Eisler, Riane, *The Chalice and the Blade, Our History, Our Future*. San Francisco: Harper & Row, 1987.

Eliot, T. S. *The Wasteland, Prufrock and Other Poems*, Mineola NY: Dover Publications, 1998.

_____ *Old Possom's Book of Practical Cats*, Boston: Hooughton Mifflin Harcourt, 2009.

Engaging Our Theological Diversity, The Commission on Appraisal, Boston: Unitarian Universalist Association, 2005.

Fahs, Sophia Lyon, *Today's Children, Yesterday's Heritage*, Boston: Beacon Press, 1952.

_____ *From Long Ago and Many Lands*, 2nd edition, Boston: Skinner House Books, 2002.

_____ in *Singing the Living Tradition*, Boston: Beacon Press, 1993, #439, #616, #657.

Ferlinghetti, Lawrence. "Oral Messages," in *A Coney Island of the Mind*, New York: New Directions Publishing Corp., pp. 52-53.

Fisher, Elizabeth, *Rise Up and Call Her Name: A Woman-honoring Journey into Global Earth-based Spiritualities*, Boston: Unitarian Universalist

Women's Federation, 1994. Reprint edition, new media, 2007. www.
riseupandcallhername.com

Flinders, Carol Lee, *At the Root of This Longing*, San Francisco: Harper,
1998.

_____ *Rebalancing the World*, New York: Harper Collins, 2002.

Friedan, Betty. *The Feminine Mystique*, New York: Norton, 2001.

Gibran, Kahlil, in *Singing the Living Tradition*, Boston: Beacon Press,
1993, #730.

Gimbutas, Marija. *Gods and Goddesses of Old Europe, 7000-3500 BC:
Myths, Legends and Cult Images*, Berkeley, CA: University of California
Press, 1974.

_____ *The Civilization of the Goddess: The World of Old Europe*, San
Francisco: Harper, 1991.

Goldberg, Natalie. *Long Quiet Highway*, New York: Bantam Books, 1993.

Hitchings, Catherine F. "Universalist and Unitarian Women Ministers,"
The Journal of the Universalist Historical Society, Vol. X, 1975.

Hocking, William Ernest in *Hymns for the Celebration of Life*, Boston:
Beacon Press, 1964, #503.

Hymns for the Celebration of Life, Boston: Beacon Press, 1964.

Ionesco, Eugene. *Rhinoceros and Other Plays*, Derek Prouse (trans.) New
York: Grove Press, 1960.

The Martin Luther King Companion, NY: St. Martin's Press, 1999.

Levy, Rachel. *The Gate of Horn: Religious Conceptions of the Stone Age and
Their Influence on European Thought*, London: Faber and Faber Ltd.,
1948.

May, Rollo. *Love and Will*. New York: W. W. Norton & Co. Inc. 1969.

Miller, Jean Baker. *Toward a New Psychology of Women*, Boston: Beacon Press, 1976.

Milne, A. A. *The Complete Tales of Winnie the Pooh*, New York: Dutton Children's Books, 1994.

Morgan, Elaine. *The Descent of Woman*, New York: Stein & Day, 1972.

Nakashima-Brock, Rita and Parker, Rebecca, "This Present Paradise," *UU World*, Vol. XXII, No. 2, Summer 2008, p. 27.

Neumann, Erich. *The Great Mother: An Analysis of the Archetype*. Bollingen Series, Princeton University Press, 1972.

Page, Shirley B. "Some Further Observations on Sin and Sickness," *Journal of Pastoral Care*, Fall, 1959.

Pagels, Elaine. *The Gnostic Gospels*, New York: Random House, 1979.

_____ "Introduction," in Burstein, Dan and De Keijzer, Arne J., eds. *Secrets of Mary Magdalene*, New York: CDS Books, 2006.

Parker, Theodore in *Singing the Living Tradition*, Boston: Beacon Press, 1993, #683.

Patai, Rafael. *The Hebrew Goddess*, NY: KTAV Publishing House, 1967.

Pirsig, Robert M. *Zen and the Art of Motorcycle Maintenance*, New York: Bantam Books, 1974.

Polanyi, Michael. *The Tacit Dimension*, Garden City, NY: Doubleday & Co., 1966.

Ranck, Shirley Ann, "100th Birthday Celebration for Sophia Lyon Fahs," *Religious Education*, New Haven, CT: Religious Education Association, Nov.-Dec. 1976, pp. 603-609.

_____ "Points of Theological Convergence Between Feminism and Post-Modern Science," *International Journal of Women's Studies*, Vol. 2, No. 4, pp. 386-397.

_____ *Cakes for the Queen of Heaven* (Curriculum), Boston: Unitarian Universalist Association, 1986.

_____ *Cakes for the Queen of Heaven: An Exploration of Women's Power Past, Present and Future*, Chicago: Delphi Press, Inc., 1995. Reprint edition: Lincoln NE: Authors Choice Press, iUniverse, Inc. 2006.

Razak, Arisika in Coleman, Monica A. "Roundtable Discussion: Must I Be Womanist?" *Journal of Feminist Studies in Religion*, 22.1, 2006, p. 100.

Rich, Adrienne. "Natural Resources," *The Dream of a Common Language: Poems 1974-1977*, New York: W. W. Norton, 1978, pp. 66-67.

Roberts, Wendy Hunter. *Celebrating Her*, Cleveland, OH: The Pilgrim Press, 1998.

Roszak, Betty. "The Spirit of the Goddess," in *Ecopsychology*, San Francisco: Sierra Club Books, 1995, pp. 297-298.

Sahtouris, Elisabet, *Gaia: The Human Journey from Chaos to Cosmos*, New York: Pocket Books, Simon & Schuster Inc., 1989.

Sarton, May. *Letters from Maine*, New York: W. W. Norton & Company, 1984.

Shlain, Leonard. *The Alphabet Versus the Goddess*, New York: Viking Penguin, 1998.

Singing the Journey, Boston: Unitarian Universalist Association, 2005.

Singing the Living Tradition, Boston: Beacon Press, 1993.

Spretnak, Charlene. *Lost Goddesses of Early Greece*, Boston: Beacon Press, 1981.

Starhawk. *The Spiral Dance: The Rebirth of the Ancient Religion of the Great Goddess*, 2nd edition, San Francisco: Harper & Row, 1989.

Stevens, Wallace. "Sunday Morning," in *Selected Poems*, John N. Serio (ed.), New York: Alfred A. Knopf, 2009, p. 42.

Stone, Merlin. *When God Was a Woman*, NY: Harcourt Brace Jovanovich, 1976.

Suzuki, D. T. "Introduction," in Herrigel, Eugen. *Zen and the Art of Archery*, New York: Pantheon Books, 1953.

_____ *Buddha of Infinite Light*, New York: Boston Shambala Publications, Random House, 1997.

Teish, Luisah "Multicolored Momma," *Jambalaya*, San Francisco: Harper & Row, 1985.

Teubal, Savina. *Sarah the Priestess*, Athens OH: Swallow Press/Ohio University Press, 1984.

Thandeka. "Healing Souls, Healing a Nation," in *A People So Bold*, Boston: Skinner House Books, 2010.

Tillich, Paul. *The Essential Tillich: An Anthology of the Writings of Paul Tillich*, F. Forester Church (ed.), New York: Macmillan, 1987.

_____ *The Courage To Be*, New Haven CT: Yale University Press, 2000.

Troeltsch, Ernst. *The Social Teaching of the Christian Churches*, O. Wyon, trans., New York: Harper & Row, 1960.

Walker, Alice. *In Search of Our Mothers' Gardens: Womanist Prose*, New York: Harcourt Brace & Company, 1983.

Walker, Barbara G. *Restoring the Goddess, Equal Rites for Modern Women*, Amherst NY: Prometheus Books, 2000.

Watts, Alan. *Eastern Wisdom, Modern Life: Collected Talks 1960-1969*. Novato CA: New World Library, 2006.

Welch, Sharon D. *Sweet Dreams in America*, New York: Routledge, 1999.

_____ *A Feminist Ethic of Risk*, Minneapolis: Fortress Press, 2000.

_____ "Audacity, Virtuosity and Wonder," in *A People So Bold*, Boston: Skinner House Books, 2010.

Wittig, Monique. *Les Guerilleres*. Trans. David Le Vey. Boston: Beacon Press, 1985.

Wordsworth, William. *Collected Poems*. Stephen Gill (ed.) New York: Oxford University Press, 2008.

Wright, Conrad. *Walking Together: Polity and Participation in Unitarian Universalist Churches*, Boston: Unitarian Universalist Association, 1989.

About the Author

A Crone of wisdom and power who has touched the lives of many women through her writing and teaching, the Reverend Shirley Ann Ranck brings both personal and professional insight to her work. Trained in education, psychology and ministry, she has drawn upon all these disciplines as well as her various personal lives as wife, mother, single parent and grandmother to create the female spiritual journey contained in *The Grandmother Galaxy.*

While working full time and birthing and raising two daughters and two sons, Shirley managed to earn her Master's degree in religious education from Drew University, an M.A. in clinical psychology from City College of New York, a Ph.D. in urban school psychology from Fordham University, and her Master of Divinity from Starr King School for the Ministry in Berkeley, California. She has been an educator and a licensed psychologist in California as well as an ordained minister in the Unitarian Universalist Association. She has worked in schools, hospitals, clinics and a county jail for women as well as in private practice.

After many years of service as a Unitarian Universalist minister, she is now retired and living in the San Francisco Bay Area where she devotes her time to writing, speaking and being an activist for women's issues and environmental concerns.